The PEER Pressure's On

In but not of the Crowd

Leader's Guide

Joy Butcher-Winfree
and
Leah Butcher-Winfree

Abingdon Press

The PEER Pressure's On

LEADER'S GUIDE

This book is printed on acid-free, recycled paper.

04 05 06 07 08 09 10 11—10 9 8 7 6 5 4 3 2

MANUFACTURED IN THE UNITED STATES OF AMERICA

Development Team
Jola Bortner
Rusty Cartee
Harriette Cross
Tim Gossett
Sharon Meads
Beth Miller
David Stewart

Editorial Team
Jenny Youngman, Editor
Pam Shepherd, Production Editor

Design Team
Keely J. Moore, Design Manager
Kelly Chinn, Designer

Administrative Staff
Neil M. Alexander, Publisher
Harriet Jane Olson, Vice President/Editor of Church School Resources
Bob Shell, Director of Youth Resources

CONTENTS

How to Use Faith in Motion

Leader Guide

Information and Formation

Topic and Key Verse
This Life-to-Bible curriculum starts with important topics for junior highs and goes to God's Word.

Take-Home Learning
The goal for the session is clear.

Younger Youth and This Topic
Find out more about your youth and how they are likely to connect with this concern.

Theology and This Topic
How does Christian faith and tradition help us to understand and deal with the concern?

You and the Scripture
Our being formed as a Christian through Bible reflection and prayer is essential for our teaching.

Transformation

The ultimate goal: Youth will become more fully devoted disciples of Jesus Christ.

Session 1

Leader's Guide

Standing on My Own

Topic: Being a Positive Peer Pressure

Scripture: Romans 12:9-10; Philippians 4:13; 1 Timothy 4:12; John 16:33

Key Verse: "Let love be genuine; hate what is evil, hold fast to what is good; love one another with mutual affection; outdo one another in showing honor" (Romans 12:9-10).

Take-Home Learning: Responding faithfully in peer pressure situations can make you an example of positive peer pressure.

Younger Youth and This Topic

Each day youth are pressured by their peers to think as their peers think and to act as their peers act. The peer pressure that today's adults experienced as youth is very different from the peer pressure today's youth confront. This pressure forces our youth to grow up faster and to make difficult decisions at an earlier age. They were not born with the skills to handle modern peer pressure, and by the time they reach pre-teen and teenage years, the pressure is extremely intense. Not only do they face society's pressure to look and act certain way, but also they are confronted with pressure from best friends, boyfriends and girlfriends, or others they wish to impress or please. They desperately need to learn skills for handling this pressure.

Youth can become positive role models for their friends while growing in their Christian faith. Sound decision-making skills and a strong faith help youth to develop good judgment as well as increase their self-esteem, their integrity, and strength of character.

Throughout this session and the following sessions, you will be helping your youth develop skills to thrive as fully-devoted disciples of Jesus Christ "in" the crowd, without becoming "of" the crowd. Jesus said that we would have trouble in this world. We can rejoice in those troubles because he has overcome the world. If they learn to think ahead and plan what they will do when facing pressure situations, they are more likely to react positively. Teach your youth IN BUT NOT OF or IBNO.

"I have told you these things, so that in me you may have peace. In this world you will have trouble. But take heart! I have overcome the world" (John 16:33, NIV).

Step Two: Be smart
The bottom line for most youth boils down to one question: Will I get in trouble? Actually, asking this question is not a bad idea! Encourage your youth to think through the consequences of their choices and to be ready to live with them. If we can help them think about the ends, we are more likely to see them thinking through the means.

Step Three: No Problem
If youth have a ready response in pressure situations, then they are less likely to make irrational decisions—because they've already thought about it and have an answer. Help your youth develop responses, truthful excuses, or reactions to pressure situations; then it will be no problem for them to do the right thing!

Step Four: Overcome
In Christ we have the power to overcome difficult situations. That doesn't mean we won't confront difficult times or that overcoming peer pressure will be easy. It does mean that we are not alone in the struggle, and that Christ's love—living in us—empowers us to be positive peer pressure!

Theology and This Topic

God created us as creative beings. As such, we inherit certain responsibilities. Although God cares for us and desires the very best for us, we still have a personal as well as social responsibility to think for ourselves, to set priorities, to establish our value systems, and to make decisions based on those priorities and values. We refer to this as *free will.* Free will does not mean that we have license to do whatever pleases us. Free will comes with a responsibility to honor God and all God's creation (our neighbors, ourselves, and the earth). That call to responsible living governs our thoughts, our decisions, and our actions. It is in being obedient to Christ's teachings and accepting the responsibility to which God has called us that we learn to stand on our own and to model positive peer pressure in "pressure" situations.

"Love from the center of who you are; don't fake it. Run for dear life from evil; hold on for dear life to good. Be good friends who love deeply; practice playing second fiddle" (Romans 12:9-10, *Message*).

You and the Scripture

Reread the key verse for this session in the margin.

- How could these words of wisdom have influenced you as an adolescent? How do they speak to you now?
- How will you convey the valuable message of the Scripture to your youth?

Think back to the days when you were a teenager. Notice the differences in society and observe the pressures our youth are experiencing. Life is more challenging than ever before. It requires courage for our youth to confront that pressure. Pray for each of your youth by name. Ask God to strengthen them and make them courageous, responsible, and bold in their faith.

Overview Chart
Look here for the big picture of the session. Also note the key activities, just in case time is tight.

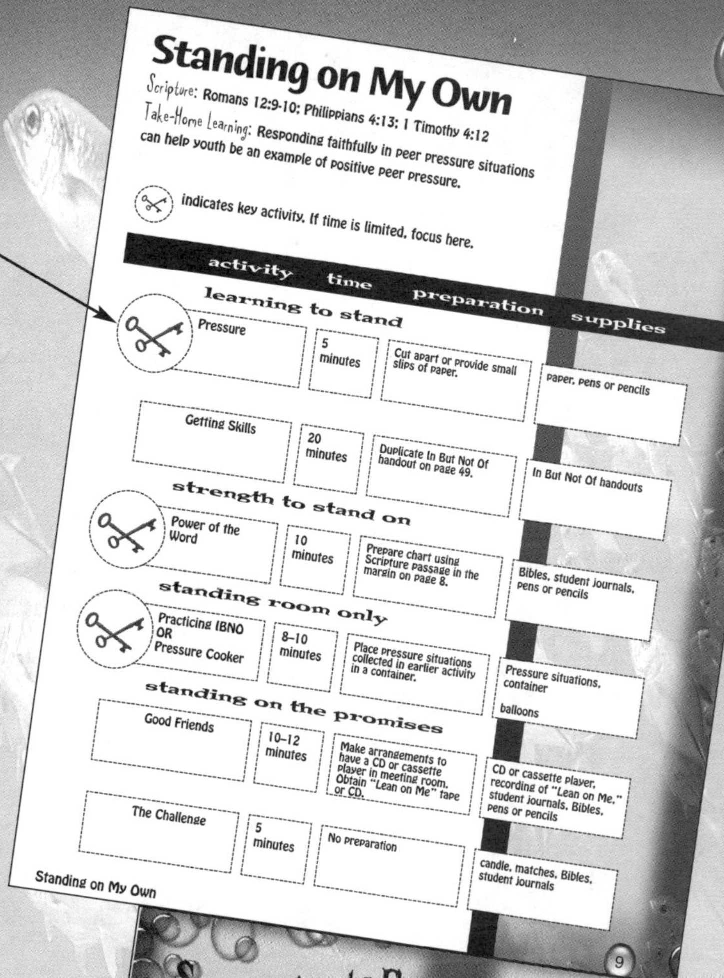

Standing on My Own

Scripture: Romans 12:9-10; Philippians 4:13; 1 Timothy 4:12

Take-Home Learning: Responding faithfully in peer pressure situations can help youth be an example of positive peer pressure.

indicates key activity. If time is limited, focus here.

activity	time	preparation	supplies
learning to stand			
Pressure	5 minutes	Cut apart or provide small slips of paper.	paper, pens or pencils
Getting Skills	20 minutes	Duplicate In But Not Of handout on page 49.	In But Not Of handouts
strength to stand on			
Power of the Word	10 minutes	Prepare chart using Scripture passage in the margin on page 8.	Bibles, student journals, pens or pencils
standing room only			
Practicing IBNO OR Pressure Cooker	8–10 minutes	Place pressure situations collected in earlier activity in a container.	Pressure situations, container balloons
standing on the promises			
Good Friends	10–12 minutes	Make arrangements to have a CD or cassette player in meeting room. Obtain "Lean on Me" tape or CD.	CD or cassette player, recording of "Lean on Me," student journals, Bibles, pens or pencils
The Challenge	5 minutes	No preparation	candle, matches, Bibles, student journals

Standing on My Own 9

Jump Right In!
The opening activity engages youth as they arrive.

Experience It!
Learning activities give youth a common base for making new connections.

Explore Connections
What do the Scriptures have to say?
What does this mean for my life?
What is a Christian to do?

Take the Challenge
The learnings are not just for Sunday!

Encounter the Holy
Ritual and mystery, prayer and commitment change hearts.

Student Journal and Reproducible Handouts

Something to Prove

It Takes Only One

Did you hear the one about the vain emperor and his new clothes? Some frauds posing as hoity-toity tailors tried to sell him on this amazing, new fabric that was so light and fine it looked invisible. The "tailors" convinced him that he was touching real fabric, even though he couldn't really feel it. (Duh! There was nothing there!) But the emperor, not wanting to appear ignorant, went along with them.

Anyway, the emperor wanted to be the first one to wear these inventive clothes, so he instructed the "tailors" to make him a new suit. These "tailors" convinced everyone that this fabric was extravagant, exquisite, and available in beautiful colors. The funny thing is that every time someone saw the fabric for the first time, they questioned whether or not they actually saw material—or just nothing at all.

When the emperor finally "tried on" his new suit, he was sure that he was naked, but since everyone told him how wonderful the suit looked, he went along with it. Onlookers didn't want to admit they didn't see anything because they were afraid of appearing stupid.

Finally, when the emperor led a parade to show off his new suit, a child yelled from the crowd, "That guy is naked!" After a few minutes, people began to realize that he really was naked. Though the emperor knew the crowd knew he was naked, he continued the farce, trying to make everyone else feel ignorant.

—Adapted from "The Emperor's New Clothes" by Hans Christian Andersen

In this story, it took only one person to speak the truth, then everyone else realized the entire situation was lie. When have you been in a situation where you were the lone voice saying, "No, this isn't right"?

12 13

Life Focus
Topics deal with issues and concerns important to junior high youth.

Spirit Forming
The journal provides practical help and scriptural encouragement.

Group Friendly
Printed Scripture references, discussion questions, and handouts facilitate participation by individuals and small groups.

Peer Pressure Rising

"Who are you?" said the Caterpillar. ... Alice replied rather shyly, "I—hardly know, sir, just at present—at least I know who I was when I got up this morning, but I have changed several times since then."

—Lewis Carroll, *Alice's Adventures in Wonderland*, 1865

Junior high youth are caught between identities. They are children and they are no longer children. They face pressure in the form of changing bodies and fragile emotions. They search for identity and look not only to their parents now, but also to friends, mentors, movies, pop stars, and magazines to answer questions like: How should I look? How should I act? More than any other age group, younger teenagers need to belong, to be accepted, to be members of a group. To find that group they try out different identities until they find the "right fit."

Trying on different identities can mean that young persons will experiment with everything from different clothes styles to piercing and makeup to dieting and sex to drugs and alcohol in order to find that place of belonging.

This is where you come in. Young persons need adults who love them and who are willing to relate to them. They need mentors who will be involved in their lives and who will care about their problems, even the ones that we think seem too small to matter! The challenge is not making quick judgments, smothering them in our infinite wisdom, or reacting with shock to the things they will tell us. They need us to show them that we really "get them"—proving by our actions that we care for them and are trying to understand what they are going through.

Everyone wants to be heard. We appreciate the feeling of being valued and important enough for someone to take the time to listen to what we have to say. So it is with junior highs. As teachers and mentors we have the opportunity to be that one to whom they turn when they need to be heard. Usually they know the answers to their problems—they just want to get it all out.

Working with junior highs places you in a very special position. You get to meet them on their level to help them discern God's truth in their lives. Consider the story of Philip and the Ethiopian. Philip was a true neighbor to the traveling Ethiopian, but more than that he was a teacher and mentor. The eunuch said something like, "I can't understand unless someone guides me." Philip sat with him and helped him understand the Scriptures. Help your youth understand the pressures they are going through by coming alongside them and grounding them in the Scriptures. Then, when the pressure mounts, they know exactly where to turn!

Blessings on you!

SESSION 1 SESSION

Standing on My Own

Topic: Being a Positive Peer Pressure

Scripture: Romans 12:9-10; Philippians 4:13; 1 Timothy 4:12; John 16:33

Key Verse: "Let love be genuine; hate what is evil, hold fast to what is good; love one another with mutual affection; outdo one another in showing honor" (Romans 12:9-10).

Take-Home Learning: Responding faithfully in peer pressure situations can make you an example of positive peer pressure.

"I have told you these things, so that in me you may have peace. In this world you will have trouble. But take heart! I have overcome the world"

(John 16:33, NIV).

Younger Youth and This Topic

Each day youth are pressured by their peers to think as their peers think and to act as their peers act. The peer pressure that today's adults experienced as youth is very different from the peer pressure today's youth confront. This pressure forces our youth to grow up faster and to make difficult decisions at an earlier age. They were not born with the skills to handle modern peer pressure, and by the time they reach pre-teen and teenage years, the pressure is extremely intense. Not only do they face society's pressure to look and act certain ways, but also they are confronted with pressure from best friends, boyfriends and girlfriends, or others they wish to impress or please. They desperately need to learn skills for handling this pressure.

Youth can become positive role models for their friends while growing in their Christian faith. Sound decision-making skills and a strong faith help youth to develop good judgment as well as to increase their self-esteem, their integrity, and strength of character.

Throughout this session and the following sessions, you will be helping your youth develop skills to thrive as fully-devoted disciples of Jesus Christ "in" the crowd, without becoming "of" the crowd. Jesus said that we would have trouble in this world. We can rejoice in those troubles because he has overcome the world. If they learn to think ahead and plan what they will do when facing pressure situations, they are more likely to react positively. Teach your youth IN BUT NOT OF or IBNO.

Step One: Investigate the situation.
Youth can learn to be aware of their surroundings and the tone of their conversations. Help them tune in to situations that may be pressurized!

Step Two: Be smart

The bottom line for most youth boils down to one question: Will I get in trouble? Actually, asking this question is not a bad idea! Encourage your youth to think through the consequences of their choices and to be ready to live with them. If we can help them think about the ends, we are more likely to see them thinking through the means.

Step Three: No Problem

If youth have a ready response in pressure situations, then they are less likely to make irrational decisions—because they've already thought about it and have an answer. Help your youth develop responses, truthful excuses, or reactions to pressure situations; then it will be no problem for them to do the right thing!

Step Four: Overcome

In Christ we have the power to overcome difficult situations. That doesn't mean we won't confront difficult times or that overcoming peer pressure will be easy. It does mean that we are not alone in the struggle, and that Christ's love—living in us—empowers us to be positive peer pressure!

Theology and This Topic

God created us as creative beings. As such, we inherit certain responsibilities. Although God cares for us and desires the very best for us, we still have a personal as well as social responsibility to think for ourselves, to set priorities, to establish our value systems, and to make decisions based on those priorities and values. We refer to this as *free will.* Free will does not mean that we have license to do whatever pleases us. Free will comes with a responsibility to honor God and all God's creation (our neighbors, ourselves, and the earth). That call to responsible living governs our thoughts, our decisions, and our actions. It is in being obedient to Christ's teachings and accepting the responsibility to which God has called us that we learn to stand on our own and to model positive peer pressure in "pressure" situations.

"Love from the center of who you are; don't fake it. Run for dear life from evil; hold on for dear life to good. Be good friends who love deeply; practice playing second fiddle"

(Romans 12:9-10, *Message).*

You and the Scripture

Reread the key verse for this session in the margin.

- How could these words of wisdom have influenced you as an adolescent? How do they speak to you now?
- How will you convey the valuable message of the Scripture to your youth?

Think back to the days when you were a teenager. Notice the differences in society and observe the pressures our youth are experiencing. Life is more challenging than ever before. It requires courage for our youth to confront that pressure. Pray for each of your youth by name. Ask God to strengthen them and make them courageous, responsible, and bold in their faith.

Standing on My Own

Scripture: Romans 12:9-10; Philippians 4:13; 1 Timothy 4:12; John 16:33

Take-Home Learning: Responding faithfully in peer pressure situations can make you be an example of positive peer pressure.

(key) indicates key activity. If time is limited, focus here.

activity	time	preparation	supplies
learning to stand			
Pressure	5 minutes	Cut apart or provide small slips of paper.	Paper, pens or pencils
(key) Getting Skills	20 minutes	Duplicate IN BUT NOT OF handout on page 49.	IN BUT NOT OF handouts
strength to stand on			
(key) Power of the Word	10 minutes	Prepare chart using Scripture passage in the margin on page 8.	Bibles, student journals, pens or pencils
standing room only			
(key) Practicing IBNO **OR** Pressure Cooker	8–10 minutes	Place pressure situations collected in earlier activity in a container.	Pressure situations, container balloons
standing on the promises			
Good Friends	10–12 minutes	Make arrangements to have a CD or cassette player in meeting room. Obtain "Lean on Me" tape or CD.	CD or cassette player, recording of "Lean on Me," student journals, Bibles, pens or pencils
The Challenge	5 minutes	No preparation	Candle, matches, Bibles, student journals

Learning to Stand

Provide slips of paper and pens or pencils.

Pressure! (5 minutes)

As youth arrive, give each a slip of paper and a pencil. Ask them to describe situations they have either experienced or heard about in which they or someone they know was being pressured to do something wrong (friends pressuring friends to harass the substitute teacher; skipping school to go to the lake; ganging up on another youth in school; drinking, and so forth). Collect these situations to use later in the session.

Getting Skills (20 minutes)

Provide copies of the IN BUT NOT OF handout (page 49).

Distribute the IN BUT NOT OF handout (page 49). Ask for some volunteers to read aloud the steps describing ways to beat peer pressure. Encourage questions and discussion. Ask:

- How would thinking through these steps help you overcome pressure situations?
- How easy or hard are these steps to accomplish?
- When have you used similar skills during peer pressure situations?

Say something like: "Later, we will use these skills to respond to the pressure situations you described earlier. These skills can help us to stand tall among the crowd of pressure. Today's Scripture verses call us to become who God desires us to be and not give in to the pressure to turn against who we know we are in Christ. We can stand tall because we know God created us to love with our whole hearts—to love God, our peers, our families, and even ourselves."

Strength to Stand On

Provide Bibles, student journals, and pens or pencils.

Power of the Word (10 minutes)

Hand out the student journals and instruct the youth to turn to page 4. Then ask for volunteers to read aloud John 16:33, Romans 12:9-10, Philippians 4:13, and 1 Timothy 4:12 as printed in their student journals. Encourage them to answer the questions in their journals. Discuss their answers by asking:

- What is each passage saying about the identity of a Christian?
- What does Romans 12:9-10 have to say about being a positive role model?
- How can you become a force for positive peer pressure?
- What changes do you need to make in your life to participate in positive peer pressure?
- Where can you receive the courage to make those changes?

Practicing IBNO (10 minutes)

Standing Room Only

Provide pressure situations collected earlier in the session and a container to hold the situations.

Place the pressure situations collected earlier in a basket or bowl.

Say: "We are going to practice the peer pressure reversal steps. Earlier in the session you provided some examples of pressure situations. I need two volunteers: one to choose a situation from the container and another to respond to the scenario using the IBNO steps. Both volunteers will roleplay the scenario and demonstrate ways we can stand on our own in peer pressure situations. Allow a few minutes for participants to think about their situations or responses before beginning the roleplay.

Ask for more volunteers to continue drawing situations from the container and to act out responses. After a few minutes of roleplaying, ask:

- How are these situations different from or similar to situations you face at school?
- On a scale of one to four (four being a lot of pressure and one being not very much pressure), how much peer pressure on these situations do you face at school and with your friends?
- How could the situations and responses have been different?
- How could IBNO help you handle pressure situations?

OR

Pressure Cooker (8–10 minutes)

Provide balloons and pressure situations collected earlier in the session and a container for the situations.

Place pressure situations collected earlier in a basket or bowl.

Divide the group into teams of two to four. Distribute to each team an equal number of roleplay situations. Now give each team a balloon. Direct each team to choose one person who will blow up the balloon while the others act as "peers." Based on the situation, the "peers" will try to persuade the person blowing up the balloon to do what they say. The one being pressured will continue blowing up the balloon as pressure mounts. (Most likely, it will become very noisy in your room!) When the balloon finally pops, the one who blew up the balloon responds to his or her "peers" using IBNO. When all balloons have popped and all situations have received responses, debrief the activity. Ask:

- Does peer pressure ever feel like a balloon about to burst? How?
- How can you respond positively to peer pressure before the situation blows up?
- How difficult is it to be a positive peer pressure in tough situations? Why?
- How is simply saying no or standing up to negative pressures acting as positive peer pressure?

Standing on the Promises

Provide Bibles, student journals, a CD or cassette player, a recording of the song "Lean on Me," and pens or pencils.

You may want to play background music with lyrics focused on friendship while youth write in their student journals. The song "Lean on Me" would be a good choice.

Good Friends (10–12 minutes)

Say something like: "Sometimes when we're in heated situations, we act without thinking. If we stopped for a moment to determine what we could do or say when faced with pressure, then we would have an advantage in tough situations. The IBNO approach can help us know what to do and say at just the right time.

"Another way we can avoid pressure situations is to surround ourselves with good friends who will stand up for us and with us and who want to help us stand tall against negative pressure. We could even surround ourselves with friends who will work with us to be positive peer pressure in our schools and hangouts." Ask:

- What are some ways to be a positive peer pressure?

Ask youth to turn to pages 6–7 in their student journals and spend some quiet time answering the questions. If possible, play the song "Lean on Me."

Provide a candle, matches, Bibles, and student journals.

The Challenge (5 minutes)

Gather youth into a circle. Place a lighted candle in the center of the group. Encourage them to spend some closing moments sharing ideas about ways they can encourage their friends and be a positive peer pressure in the coming week. (If they are slow to volunteer ideas, suggest the following: If a fellow student is struggling in a subject you understand, offer to study with him. Or, stick up for someone who needs a friend.) Say, "Offering these petitions aloud is a way to ask for God's help and to pray for one another in specific ways."

When everyone has talked, ask the group to say aloud together the prayer written in their student journals on page 7: "Lord, help us to stand strong in our faith and to be positive influences in hard situations." Close with a prayer for your youth.

Session 2

Oh, To Be Popular!

Topic: Belonging, Cliques, and Shunning: The Price of Being Popular

Scripture: Luke 9:25; Proverbs 13:20

Key Verse: "What does it profit them if they gain the whole world, but lose or forfeit themselves?" (Luke 9:25).

Take-Home Learning: Because you belong to God, you are accepted by the One who really matters.

Younger Youth and This Topic

Popularity is important to most teens. Being a part of the "in" crowd is often something teens find appealing. If they are not part of the "in" crowd during junior high or middle school years, many basically feel "out" and unpopular. In their efforts to become popular, teens may express themselves in unusual ways. We can teach our teens to find their confidence in God, to be true to their faith, and to cultivate genuine friendships. Often teens who belong to the "popular" crowd are overly stressed and don't fully explore the principles of genuine friendship. Some youth may believe that if they don't do what other youth are doing, they will lose the opportunity to make friends.

Think of cliques in terms of power and control rather than friendship. Since most teens at this age feel insecure, they struggle with issues of acceptance. Some youth try to put aside their own negative self-images by controlling others. Others attempt to make themselves feel better at another person's expense, ridiculing his or her shortcomings. Typically, boys are categorized as bullies; however, hostility between girls often surfaces during the middle school years in the form of backstabbing, belittling, and intimidating behavior. Teens who have been the victims of rumors, the silent treatment, ostracism, and ridicule often feel as badly as if they had been physically attacked. At such a fragile age, the hurt suffered from rumors and ridicule is observed in poor body-image, low to no self-esteem, and for some, even fatal consequences.

As youth leaders and teachers, you are role models along with their parents and peers. One of your responsibilities is to provide love and support. Youth will learn by watching you interact with members of your own group as well as outsiders.

Consider the following questions in regards to the composition of your group:

- Who are the youth that appear to be members of the "in" crowd?
- Who are the youth that do not seem to be members of any group or crowd?

Theology and This Topic

Popularity and the issues surrounding popularity—belonging, shunning others to make one feel better about his or her own shortcomings—raise significant theological issues. We have an inherent need to belong. We were created to be in relationship with the Creator and with others. Therefore, it is natural for human beings to desire being known, accepted, and loved. The essence of the biblical story is that human beings experience a covenant relationship with God which includes both our falling away and our journey back to God. God never lets us go, and this covenant God has made with us cannot be broken. God knows our need to be in relationship even before we ourselves become aware of that need. The dilemma of living in the world but not of the world continues to plague us. As Christians, we struggle to maintain Christian ideals and values in a culture that seduces us to obtain what we desire regardless of what we must do to obtain it or of others' feelings. This struggle is evidence of our sinfulness. Our social culture sets the norms for what looks good, how we act, what we should possess, and attempts to make a claim on our loyalties. It is very difficult to be who we are in the midst of this struggle. It is even more difficult for teenagers who are just beginning to discover their own Christian identities. We can, however, overcome this force by fully understanding whose we are and grasping the lasting claim that God has made on our lives.

You and the Scripture

"What good would it do to get everything you want and lose you, the real you?"

(Luke 9:25, *Message*).

Read the Scripture in the margin. Can you recall your middle school years and your own social struggles and humiliations? Were you popular? Were you part of the "in" crowd? Were you a member of a clique? Were you shunned in your social system? Who did the shunning? Do you have a social memory, painful or otherwise, that you've suppressed? Consider sharing these recollections with your youth.

- What good would it do to obtain everything you desire yet lose the real you?
- In what areas of your life do you struggle with wanting to be like your peers?
- What do you feel you must do to be accepted and liked?
- What parts of you have been lost as a result of your need to be accepted?

Pray that God would shine into those dark places of loneliness and weakness so that you might become strong.

Oh, To Be Popular!

Scripture: Luke 9:25; Proverbs 13:20

Take-Home Learning: Because you belong to God, you are accepted by the One who really matters.

(key icon) indicates key activity. If time is limited, focus here.

activity	time	preparation	supplies
learning to stand			
(key) What's Cool? **AND** In or Out	5 minutes 8–10 minutes	Collect a variety of teen magazines. Arrange chairs in a circle.	Magazines, large sheet of paper or posterboard, glue, scissors
Think About It	5–8 minutes	No preparation	Bibles, student journals, pens or pencils
strength to stand on			
Celebrate Us! Who Says It's Cool?	5 minutes 10 minutes	No preparation	Student journals, pens or pencils Collage from What's Cool? activity on page 16.
(key) Cool Like Jesus What Makes You Different …	5 minutes 10 minutes	No preparation Prepare a chart of Luke 9:25 and Proverbs 13:20.	Student journals, pens or pencils Large sheet of paper, marker
standing room only			
(key) Practicing IBNO	10 minutes	Duplicate Making a Difference handout (page 50).	Making a Difference handout (page 50), pencils, IBNO handout (page 49)
standing on the promises			
The Challenge	5 minutes	No preparation	Candle and matches

Learning to Stand

Provide a large sheet of paper or posterboard, glue, scissors, and a variety of teen magazines.

What's Cool? (5 minutes)

As youth arrive, have them peruse magazines to find and cut out pictures of items they consider to be "cool" (clothes, activities, pictures of girls, boys, places, cars, and so forth). Instruct them to glue or tape pictures in collage fashion to a large sheet of paper or posterboard and to think about why they believe these items are cool and who says they are cool!

AND

Arrange chairs in a circle.

In or Out (8–10 minutes)

Help the youth begin to wrestle with the issue of popularity and the feelings of being on the outside. Gather youth in a circle and ask for two or three volunteers. Have the volunteers leave the room and discuss with remaining youth what kind of group they want to be. Choose some sort of commonality such as wearing a certain type of clothing, playing a certain sport, attending the same school, and so forth.

Bring the volunteers back into the room and ask them to try to guess the identity of the "in crowd." They may ask only yes or no questions, one at a time.

When the "outsiders" guess incorrectly, the "insider's" response should be, "Nope, you're out!" If a volunteer guesses correctly, then he or she is brought into the circle while the other volunteers go back out of the room and the game begins again.

Play for about ten minutes or until all of the "outsiders" have made it into the "in crowd." Then debrief the activity by asking the "outsiders" to describe their feelings as a result of not being a part of the group.

Provide Bibles, student journals, and pens or pencils.

Think About It (5–8 minutes)

Distribute the student journals and ask youth to turn to page 8. Ask them to answer the questions with a partner. When it looks like the partners are having some good discussions, call the group back together and discuss their answers.

- What is a clique?
- What cliques are in your school or church? What are they like?
- Are cliques ever good? When?
- Are you a member of a clique? Are you happy with your group of friends? Why do you get along well?
- In your clique, how do you decide who gets in and who doesn't?

- How does it feel to not be "in"?
- Who are the people who are not "in"? Are they bullied or harassed? When have you been bullied or harassed?
- What do you think about kids who hurt other kids by bullying or teasing them?
- What happens if someone reaches out to rescue a bullied peer?

Celebrate Us! (5 minutes)

Have the youth pair up to talk through the questions on page 9 in the student journal. After a few minutes, bring the group back together and ask, "How does God feel about popularity?"

Who Says It's Cool? (10 minutes)

Strength to Stand On

Provide the collage youth made earlier in the What's Cool? activity on page 16.

Ask youth to look at the collage they created earlier in the session and to identify and explain their individual contributions by answering the following: Why do you think this item/place is cool? Who says it's cool?

Discuss:

- Do all your friends feel the same way you do about the clothes you wear? the activities in which you participate? the places you go?
- What happens if you don't do what your friends do or don't like what they like or don't wear what they wear?
- Why do you think we often let other people tell us who we are?

Have the youth work individually to answer the questions on page 10 in their student journals. Then discuss the true/false statement: If you don't love yourself, it's impossible to love others.

Cool Like Jesus (5 minutes)

Tell the youth to answer the questions on page 10 in their student journals. Then have them draw pictures or symbols in the boxes to explain their answers. Ask for volunteers to talk about their pictures.

Provide a large sheet of paper, marker, student journals, and pens or pencils.

Before the session, prepare a chart displaying Luke 9:25 and Proverbs 13:20.

Remember, youth don't always need to respond aloud. Point out that they may continue to wrestle with these questions as they grow older.

What Makes You Different … Makes You Beautiful! (10 minutes)

Read aloud together Luke 9:25 and Proverbs 13:20 using the chart you prepared earlier. Then read aloud Luke 9:25 (*Message*) on page 14.

Leader's Guide

Ask and discuss the following questions:

- What do these passages mean to you?
- What good would it be if you gained the whole world—all kinds of popularity—but lost yourself along the way?
- How does this passage help us to think about the importance of popularity?
- Is popularity important to you? Why or why not?
- What kind of popularity would make you happy?
- What kids are popular at school? Would you want to be like them if you could? What would you have to change about yourself to make that happen?
- What would Jesus say about changing yourself to fit in?

Talk through the questions in the student journal on page 11. Spend some time discussing God's love for us. Say, "Regardless of our level of popularity, we are always "in" and beautiful to God." Ask, "What's your prayer about popularity?"

Standing Room Only

Provide Making a Difference handout (page 50) and pencils. You may want to have available additional copies of the IBNO handout (page 49).

Practicing IBNO (10 minutes)

Distribute the Making a Difference handouts (page 50) and pens. Explain that they will practice IBNO as it relates to popularity. Encourage them to refer to the IBNO handout (page 49) used in session one.

Divide youth into small groups or pairs and direct them to complete the story using the IBNO steps. When the groups are finished, ask each group to choose one person to tell the group's story.

Standing on the Promises

Provide a candle and matches.

The Challenge (5 minutes)

Ask youth to form a circle. Place a lighted candle in the middle of the group. Say: "This week notice the youth who are left out—those who are loners. Make an attempt to speak to them; ask them to sit with you at lunch; make a point to learn about them."

Ask youth to spend closing moments sharing thoughts and ideas about ways they intend to reach out to those who are left out of their cliques and crowds. Help them to understand that verbalizing their intent is one way to ask for God's help and to enlist their friends' prayer support in specific ways. Ask the group to respond to each youth's comment by saying aloud together: "Lord, help us to be compassionate." Close with a prayer for your youth.

SESSION 3

Something to Prove

Topic: When Peers Encourage Peers to Lie, Cheat, and Steal

Scripture: Matthew 22:34-40; Exodus 20:15-16; Luke 6:31

Key Verse: "'You shall love the Lord your God with all your heart, and with all your soul, and with all your mind.' This is the greatest and first commandment. And a second is like it: 'You shall love your neighbor as yourself'" (Matthew 22:37-39).

Take-Home Learning: We can live with honesty and integrity, even when pressured on all sides to do just the opposite.

Younger Youth and This Topic

Teens have many decisions to make: choosing friends; deciding hobbies or extracurricular activities; how to dress, act, or be; and so on. Their desire is to make these types of decisions on their own. The toughest decisions involve peer pressure. As youth leaders, it is important to understand the power of peer approval.

Peers influence one another's lives by simply spending time together. Pressure occurs when peers verbally or non-verbally encourage their friends to act as they act, do as they do, and think as they think.

We can help young persons become thinkers and teach them to make good decisions. Lying, cheating, and stealing are obviously bad decisions. We can help youth develop a sense of honesty and integrity so that even in junior high they can do the right thing! Younger teens are very prone to go along with the crowd, but in these areas especially, they have a sense of right and wrong. Helping them to learn integrity early on can motivate them to think for themselves, go against the crowd, and remember that honesty is usually the best policy (cliché or not!).

Research indicates that peer pressure influences teens to change their own opinions (even when they know them to be valid) because others give incorrect or untruthful answers. The opposite is true as well: If just one person is able to say what they know to be true, it encourages everyone else to speak the truth. Consider the story of the emperor's new clothes. It took only one person to speak up and say: "Wait a minute! He's naked! Those aren't new clothes!" Then everyone else observed the truth as well. If we can help youth to speak up despite what others say, they can become a positive force and free others to speak the truth. It is important

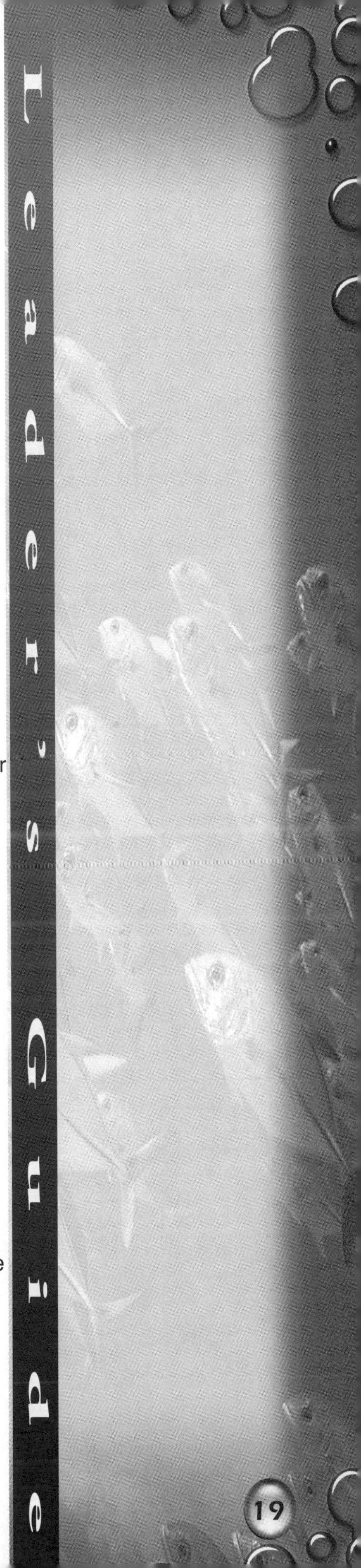

to help our youth recognize that when they make bad decisions—such as lying, stealing, or cheating—they may be allowing the influences of others to keep them from thinking for themselves. Youth find it difficult to say no to their peers because they are afraid they won't be liked or accepted and ultimately will be dropped as friends. Youth are afraid of rejection—and so are adults.

Theology and This Topic

The first response to thinking about these topics would probably be the Ten Commandments. God gave us these commandments to live by. However, junior highers especially may not take a simple "thou shalt not" answer when wrestling with peer pressure topics. They may question if lying is appropriate or wonder: "Is working together on homework technically cheating, or is downloading music illegally really stealing?"

Jesus teaches us that the "bottom line" of the Ten Commandments is to love God above all and to love others as much as we love ourselves. When we go outside the boundaries God set for us, we can't truly love God with our hearts, souls, and minds or truly love our neighbors. We can help teenagers understand that lying, cheating, and stealing are actions that take away from our loving God, loving others, and loving ourselves. In performing these actions, we take a step away from God.

It's important to remember that God knows our shortcomings and failures and offers forgiveness even when we are undeserving. God never takes a step away from us. It's what believers understand and know as *grace*. But we do not experience this grace until we come face-to-face with the actions and behaviors that go against our loving God. Grace is fully experienced when we confess our wrongdoings and seek to change our behavior. Then we can choose attitudes and behaviors that are pleasing to God. Admittedly, often we are unaware of such behaviors because we have not learned them. It is in the process of growing up, making mistakes, and receiving forgiveness that we learn to value life and one another.

Read **Matthew 22:37-39.**

God be in my head, and in my understanding;
God be in my eyes, and in my looking;
God be in my mouth, and in my speaking;
God be in my heart, and in my thinking;
God be at mine end, and in my departing.

Sarum Primer, 1558

You and the Scripture

Read the key Scripture referenced in the margin and examine the ways in which you express your love for God and neighbor.

Adults are not too old to be influenced by peer pressure. As you prepare for this session, consider that the issues related to this topic (lying, cheating, and stealing) are appropriate for adults and not "for kids only." For example, adults often think nothing of telling "a little white lie" (social lying), if we do not want to be publicly embarrassed or if we do not want to hurt someone's feelings by saying what we really think. As you pray and prepare for this session, ask God to bring to mind specific issues which apply to your own life. Pray the *Sarum Primer* as a way of giving yourself fully to God.

Something to Prove

Scripture: Exodus 20:15-16; Luke 6:31

Take-Home Learning: We can live with honesty and integrity, even when pressured on all sides to do just the opposite.

(key icon) indicates key activity. If time is limited, focus here.

activity	time	preparation	supplies
learning to stand			
Famous Peer Pressure Lines	5 minutes	No preparation	Large sheet of paper or posterboard, markers
(key) What Would You Say? Debrief	5–10 minutes 5 minutes	Prepare and display three signs (see page 22). Duplicate and cut apart handouts.	Paper, markers, Feeling the Pressure handout (page 51)
strength to stand on			
(key) Integrity 101	15–20 minutes	Prepare a chart defining the word *integrity.*	Large sheet of paper and markers, student journals, pens or pencils
Responding to Pressure	5–10 minutes	No preparation	Student journals, pens or pencils
standing room only			
(key) Practicing IBNO	10 minutes	No preparation	Feeling the Pressure handout (page 51), large sheet of paper, marker
standing on the promises			
"Help!" The Challenge	10 minutes 5 minutes	Obtain a CD or cassette player. No preparation	Bibles, student journals, CDs or cassettes, pens or pencils Candles and matches

Leader's Guide

Learning to Stand

Provide a large sheet of paper or posterboard and markers.

Provide markers, paper for signs, and Feeling the Pressure handouts (page 51).

Prepare three signs that say: (1) Absolutely No! (2) Absolutely Yes! and (3) Maybe. Display each one on a different wall in the meeting room.

Duplicate and cut apart the Feeling the Pressure handout on page 51.

Famous Peer Pressure Lines! (5 minutes)

As youth arrive, direct them to the large sheet of paper or posterboard and instruct them to write two statements: (1) the "line" they hear most often from their peers when they want them to do something they know they shouldn't or that might result in negative consequences; (2) the request that might go along with the "line." Share an example such as "No one will ever know" and "Come on, let's skip class."

What Would You Say? (5–10 minutes)

Point out the signs you prepared and posted earlier. Say: "It takes courage and willpower to say no to your peers."

Ask for a volunteer to help you demonstrate the principle of saying no. Explain that you will read aloud a scenario that a peer might suggest. Ask the volunteer to indicate his or her response to the situation by moving to stand by the appropriate response sign: Absolutely No!, Yes! or Maybe.

Before reading aloud scenario one, distribute the bottom half of the Feeling the Pressure handout to the remaining youth and instruct them to pressure the volunteer to change his or her mind by using the lines printed on the handout or the lines they wrote on the large sheet of paper as they arrived. Encourage youth to be persistent, persuasive, and dramatic in their pressure.

Read aloud the first scenario. Wait for the volunteer to stand near the poster indicating his or her response, then give notice for remaining youth to begin the peer pressure. After a minute or two, ask for another volunteer. Follow the same procedure for scenarios two and three.

AND

Debrief (5 minutes)

Ask the volunteers, "How did it feel to be under so much pressure?" If the volunteers changed their minds under pressure, discuss the reasons why. Then ask the remaining youth how it felt to apply the pressure. Discuss reasons teens on both sides of the scenario might have changed their minds.

Strength to Stand On

Provide a large sheet of paper and markers.

Prepare a chart using the definition for *integrity* at the top of page 23.

Integrity 101 (15–20 minutes)

Say: "As we talk about the topics for the day, we'll keep coming back to what it means to have integrity. So before we talk about what we don't want to do, let's define what we do want."

As you discuss the following questions, post the chart you prepared earlier with a definition of the word *integrity*.

Ask:

- What do you think the word *integrity* means?
- When have you previously heard the word *integrity*?

Say: "Integrity basically means doing what you know to be right, even when no one is watching or when the potential for getting caught doesn't matter—when it's just you doing the right thing because you know it's the right thing to do." Ask:

- Based on this definition, when have you acted with integrity?
- Don't respond aloud, but think of some decisions you've made that didn't demonstrate integrity.

Read aloud together Matthew 22:37 from the student journal (page 14). Then ask:

Provide student journals and pens or pencils.

- What do you think this passage has to do with honesty and integrity?
- How can loving God and others help us to do the right thing—to have integrity?

Now read aloud Exodus 20:15-16.

- What boundaries does God set for us in these verses?
- In what ways are lying, cheating, and stealing similar?
- How can they be harmful actions?

Now read aloud Luke 6:31 and discuss the following:

- How would you feel if you were the storeowner in scenario one?
- How would you feel if you were the one asking to cheat using your friend's homework in scenario two?
- How would you feel if you were your parents and your child lied to you as occurred in scenario three?

Say: "When we go outside the boundaries that God set for us, we are not fully loving God nor our neighbors. God set those boundaries for us so that we wouldn't harm others and so that we would love them. God doesn't just say, 'Don't do this' and 'Don't do that.' God wants us to take on Christ's character—to love God with our whole selves and to love our neighbors as much as we love ourselves. God also wants our actions to be expressions of that love—to be honest and to demonstrate integrity."

Responding to Pressure (5–10 minutes)

Direct the youth to work individually on "Responding to Pressure" questions in the student journal (page 14). After a few minutes, invite volunteers to share anything they might have learned about themselves.

Standing Room Only

Provide the Feeling the Pressure handout (page 51), a large sheet of paper, and markers.

Practicing IBNO (10 minutes)

Refer again to the scenarios on the Feeling the Pressure handout. For each scenario, direct youth to work through IBNO. Center the bulk of your discussion time around "Be Smart," helping youth to consider the consequences on this side of a possible problem. List their responses on a large sheet of paper. Ask and discuss:

- What could happen if you gave in to the peer pressure and participated in the negative behaviors these scenarios describe?

The following are some possible consequences (if they are not mentioned by teens):

- *Shoplifting: youth may not be allowed in store again; possible arrest; loss of privileges at home, school, and church.*
- *Lying: loss of parents' trust; possibility of accident occurring during the concert.*
- *Cheating: both students receive a failing grade; incident recorded on permanent record; loss of trust by teacher as well as by parents.*

Discuss other examples of lying, cheating, and stealing that, on the surface, may not appear to be as severe a crime (*stealing from parents or friends; lying about sneaking out at night, skipping school, gossip; cheating by forging a parent's signature on permission forms or report cards*).

Standing on the Promises

Provide Bibles, student journals, pens or pencils, and CDs or cassettes.

Play soft background music while students write their prayers.

"Help!" (10 minutes)

Have students write a prayer of confession in their student journals (page 15). Encourage them to use the prayer promptings as a guide for talking with God.

They may struggle with how to respond to the promptings if they have never lied, cheated on a test, or stolen something from a store. Help them look beyond these types of incidents to any form of dishonesty in their lives. Assure them of God's forgiveness, grace, mercy, and love.

Provide a candle and matches.

The Challenge (5 minutes)

Direct youth to form a circle. Place a lighted candle in the middle of the circle. Ask youth to spend a few moments thinking of ways they can respond lovingly to friends who pressure them in negative ways during the coming week. Ask those who are willing to share their ideas. Encourage them to say their petitions aloud. After each teen shares, ask the group to say aloud together: "Lord, give us strength." Close with a prayer for your youth and their plans to make a positive difference among their peers.

SESSION 4

Going Too Far

Topic: Sex, Partying, and Self-Control

Scripture: 1 Peter 4:1-5; 1 Corinthians 6:12-20; Ephesians 4:17-19

Key Verses: "You have already spent enough time in doing what the Gentiles like to do, living in licentiousness, passions, drunkenness, revels, carousing, and lawless idolatry. They are surprised that you no longer join them in the same excesses of dissipation, and so they blaspheme" (1 Peter 4:3-4).

"Shun fornication! Every sin that a person commits is outside the body; but the fornicator sins against the body itself. Or do you not know that your body is a temple of the Holy Spirit within you, which you have from God, and that you are not your own?" (1 Corinthians 6:18-19).

Take-Home Learning: We are created by God to be beautiful, sexual beings and with that comes a responsibility to exercise self-control and seek purity as a temple for the Holy Spirit.

Younger Youth and This Topic

Sexuality is one of God's most beautiful gifts. By the time youth reach adolescence, they are very aware of their own and others' sexuality, although they may not fully understand the beauty in it yet. They have been introduced to the topic by their friends, television, movies, music, advertising, the Internet, books, and magazines. Sexuality, in some form, influences nearly every aspect of teenagers' lives.

Because teens are bombarded with sex, it is all the more important to help them develop a clear sense of who they are as created, sexual beings and to help them set clear and uncompromising boundaries for themselves. Many parents, though they may find it uncomfortable to talk with their children about sex, have begun the conversations. Most likely, youth also have attended classes in school dealing with the subject. In this session, you can help them tie together all of the information they have learned with conversations they have had and to view their sexuality from a faith perspective.

Parties are important for teenagers, but parties are also places where boundaries are blurred and it becomes much easier to compromise. Most stories of regret are the result of actions at a party the previous weekend. Teens need to feel a part of the group and together enjoy times of fun and release. They also need to establish a strong sense of self-control and

"You've already put in your time in that God-ignorant way of life, partying night after night, a drunken and profligate life. ... Of course, your old friends don't understand" (1 Peter 4:3-4, *Message*).

"In sexual sin we violate the sacredness of our own bodies, these bodies that were made for God-given and God-modeled love" (1 Corinthians 6:18-19, *Message*).

self-respect so that they don't go with the flow when confronted with pressure situations.

Factual data adapted from information researched by The Alan Guttmacher Institute (1999) and The National Campaign to Prevent Teen Pregnancy (1999).

Every year in the United States approximately one million teenagers become pregnant and three million teenagers contract a sexually transmitted disease. Likely, these statistics are much greater for individuals who are uneducated about sex. The adolescent pregnancy rate in the United States continues to be the highest in the industrialized world. Most effective teen pregnancy prevention programs include education related to reproductive health, skills, abstinence, and availability of contraception. Many include activities that seek to nurture in teens a sense of confidence and a hope for the future.

A common reason teens have sex is that their boyfriends or girlfriends pressure them, and so to keep from losing their boyfriends or girlfriends, they have sex before they are ready. Some teens even engage in competition with their peers to acquire multiple sexual partners. Others try everything but intercourse—from oral sex to mutual masturbation—not equating these acts as "sex." Teens engaging in sex before they are emotionally ready can result in low self-esteem, the feeling of being used, and a fear of pregnancy or sexually transmitted disease. Many teens believe that everyone is doing it. The truth is that about one in five young people do not have intercourse while teenagers. Some youth claim to be sexually active when they aren't and only want to find their place in the "in crowd."

Theology and This Topic

Within the context of marriage, sex is a beautiful gift from God. Scripture teaches that sexual relations are meant to be part of a deep relationship of love and commitment—not only for reproduction but for bonding, love, and enjoyment. As Paul describes the role of sexuality in marriage, it is clear that the full expression of our physical desires—sexual intercourse—is to be reserved for the marriage relationship. In contradiction to the world's attitude that says, "If it feels good do it," Paul teaches God's call to exercise control over our passions and our bodies in the area of premarital sex. When we become Christians, we dedicate ourselves to the Lord. Our bodies are no longer only ours but become God's temple.

You and the Scripture

Read **Ephesians 4:16.**

As youth leaders, sharing is an expression of our love. God gives each of us different gifts and by sharing those gifts with others, we experience the full range of God's blessings. When we share, we connect with others in relationship and demonstrate our Christian love.

As you pray and prepare for this session, ask God to reveal those areas where you might be uncomfortable. Ask God to give you strength and wisdom to discern the appropriate words that invite inquiry and trust from your youth. Don't be afraid to address issues that may not have been addressed by your youth's parents. As a youth leader, you play an extremely important role in helping to nurture healthy and loving teens.

Going Too Far

Scripture: 1 Peter 4:1-5; 1 Corinthians 6:12-20; Ephesians 4:17-19

Take-Home Learning: We are created by God to be beautiful, sexual beings and with that comes a responsibility to exercise self-control and seek purity as a temple for the Holy Spirit.

(key) indicates key activity. If time is limited, focus here.

activity	time	preparation	supplies
strength to stand			
What's My Line?	5 minutes	No preparation	Large sheet of paper, markers, tape
(key) Practicing IBNO **AND** Debrief	10–15 minutes 10 minutes	Duplicate Party Time Scenario (page 52). No preparation	Party Time Scenario handout, paper, pens, large sheet of paper, marker
strength to stand on			
(key) God-modeled Love	10 minutes	Prepare a chart with phrases for belief statement.	Student journals, Bibles, paper, pens, large sheet of paper, marker
standing room only			
(key) Party Rules	10 minutes	No preparation	Large sheet of paper, markers
standing on the promises			
What's It All About?	10 minutes	No preparation	Bibles, student journals, pens
The Challenge	5 minutes	No preparation	Candle and matches

Learning to Stand

Provide a large sheet of paper, markers, and tape.

What's My Line? (5 minutes)

As youth arrive, direct them to write on the large sheet of paper in graffiti style a "pressure" line that might be used to persuade someone to have sex. After all youth have contributed their lines, ask them to vote on the most used or most absurd "pressure line."

Suggest some lines that might not have been mentioned:

- "If you really love me, you'd do this with me."
- "You don't understand. It really hurts me to stop now."
- "You're beautiful and sexy. You really turn me on."
- "Why won't you do it with me? Are you a prude?"
- "You're a real tease. I thought you wanted to."
- "Don't be scared. You can't get pregnant the first time."
- "If I had AIDS, you could tell."
- "No one will find out."
- "Everyone is doing it."

Provide Party Time Scenario handout (page 52), paper, and pens.

Duplicate the Party Time Scenario handout (page 52).

Practicing IBNO (10–15 minutes)

Read aloud the Party Time Scenario (page 52). After reading aloud the story about Cindy, distribute a handout to each youth. Then divide youth into small groups. (If you are a small group, assign more than one instruction to pairs.) Give the following assignments to each group. Allow five to seven minutes for group work.

Group One (I): Identify and circle the "pressure lines" or points of pressure in the scenario.

Group Two (B): Identify and underline the rules that were broken.

Group Three (B): List the possible and real consequences for the youth depicted in this illustration.

Group Four (N): List alternate actions for avoiding the outcome.

Group Five (O) List some possible responses that could have helped Kaitlyn exit the high-pressure situation. What are some Scriptures that she could rely on in this situation?

AND

Debrief (10 minutes)

Provide a large sheet of paper and marker.

List group responses on a large sheet of paper. Then discuss:

- How do you think Kaitlyn felt?
- How would you have felt?
- How might Cindy feel?
- Was there any love or commitment revealed in the story?

God-modeled Love (10 minutes)

Divide youth into three small groups and assign each group to answer one of the following sets of Scriptures and discussion questions (see student journal, pages 16–17).

Group One: 1 Peter 4:3-5
Key Verse: "You've already put in your time in that God-ignorant way of life, partying night after night, a drunken and profligate life. Now it's time to be done with it for good. Of course, your old friends don't understand why you don't join in with the old gang anymore. But you don't have to give an account to them" (*Message*).

- What does this passage say about peer pressure?
- What does this passage say about going too far?
- Are parties wrong?

Group Two: 1 Corinthians 6:18-19
Key Verse: "We must not pursue the kind of sex that avoids commitment and intimacy, leaving us more lonely than ever—the kind of sex that can never 'become one.' … In sexual sin we violate the sacredness of our own bodies, these bodies that were made for God-given and God-modeled love, for 'becoming one' with another" (*Message*).

- What does this passage say about peer pressure?
- What does this passage say about going too far?
- What does this passage say about sex?

Group Three: Ephesians 4:17-19
Key Verse: "And so I insist—and God backs me up on this—that there be no going along with the crowd, the empty-headed, mindless crowd. … Feeling no pain, they let themselves go in sexual obsession" (*Message*).

- What does this passage say about peer pressure?
- What does this passage say about going too far?
- What does this passage say about partying and sex?

Reassemble the small groups and ask each group to read aloud its assigned passage and present conclusions and answers. Then instruct youth to compose a statement of belief based on what they learned by studying the Scriptures. To get them started, call attention to the chart you prepared earlier listing possible beginnings to a belief statement:

We believe that God created us …

We believe that God thinks sex is …

We believe that our bodies …

We believe that we should care for our bodies by …

We believe that we can …

Strength to Stand On

Provide Bibles, student journals, paper, and pens.

Provide a large sheet of paper or posterboard and a marker.

Prepare a chart listing possible beginnings to a belief statement.

Standing Room Only

Provide a large sheet of paper and markers.

Party Rules (10 minutes)

Ask the group to determine and list rules for a hypothetical party. Explain that these might be rules they discuss with their parents for parties at home or they might be rules they agree on for attending parties elsewhere. To help the group begin, suggest these discussion starters: What rooms of the house will be used? What activities are unacceptable? Should parents be at home during the entire party? Will it be an open invitation or written invitations? How many people will be invited? What type of food and drinks will be served? What are the consequences for use of alcohol, drugs, or cigarettes? What sort of music will be played and at what volume level? Will friends be allowed to leave and return? Will you alert neighbors in advance? What is a reasonable ending time for the party? How will you turn down an invitation to or leave a party where these rules are being broken?

Discuss how self-control might be necessary at a party? Ask:

- How easy is it to just "go with the flow" at a party?
- Why do some people lose all sense of self-control in party situations?
- How can you enjoy a party without compromising your self-respect or your faith?

Encourage youth, if they haven't already, to talk to their parents about boundaries concerning parties and activities that occur when their parents aren't around. Help them to think about seriously and respect the rules their parents set for them.

Standing on the Promises

Provide Bibles, student journals, and pens.

What's It All About? (10 minutes)

Encourage youth to spend a few minutes individually answering the "What's It All About?" questions in their student journals (page 18). After a few minutes, invite volunteers to share any insights they learned about themselves or new decisions they might have made concerning sex.

Provide a candle and matches.

The Challenge (5 minutes)

Ask youth to form a circle. Place a lighted candle in the middle of the circle. Invite youth to spend a few closing moments sharing thoughts about ways they will respond this week to friends who pressure them in a negative way. Remind youth that this is one way to ask for God's help and to share specific prayer needs with their friends. After each youth shares, ask the group to say aloud together: "Lord, help us to celebrate your Spirit in us." Close with a prayer for your youth and their struggles for self-control.

Session 5

Getting Hooked

Topic: Addictions: Alcohol, Smoking, and Drugs

Scripture: 1 Corinthians: 3:16-17; 1 John 2:15-17; Luke 21:34

Key Verse: "Do you not know that you are God's temple and that God's Spirit dwells in you? If anyone destroys God's temple, God will destroy that person. For God's temple is holy, and you are that temple" (1 Corinthians 3:16-17).

Take-Home Learning: Addictive behaviors can have long-term, even deadly, effects on our physical, emotional, and spiritual lives.

"You realize, don't you, that you are the temple of God, and God himself is present in you? No one will get by with vandalizing God's temple, you can be sure of that. God's temple is sacred—and you, remember, *are* the temple" (1 Corinthians 3:16-17, *Message*).

Younger Youth and This Topic

We live in a drug-using society. Early on, youth take prescription medicines as well as "over-the-counter" cough medicines. They are exposed to family members who smoke, drink alcohol, and take drugs for medical purposes as well as for "recreational" purposes. They continue to receive conflicting messages from television shows, movies, and advertising. However, recent studies by Partnership for a Drug-Free America document that drug use among teens is leveling off and/or declining because parents are talking with their children about drugs. Drug and alcohol use is an important topic—one that needs to be addressed from all directions. It is crucial that our youth understand that drugs are chemicals that change the way our bodies work, and some drugs kill brain cells that never can be replaced.

Why do our kids use these dangerous drugs? Among the many reasons, these are the most named among teenagers: they see older kids using and want to be like them; they are curious; they are sad, scared, or bored; they want to forget their problems; they want to fit in with their friends; they believe using will make them cool; they want their parents' attention; their family members use; television shows, movies, and advertising make it appear fun; they believe it helps them to loosen up in social situations.

If teens *try* drugs for the reasons above, then why do they *keep using*? They want to continue to be a part of the crowd—to find a sense of belonging. They may keep using to show they can make their own decisions or because they like the feelings that come from using. Teens who tend to be anxious use drugs to feel some relief from stress. In emotionally repressed teens, drugs may help them to express their feelings more freely. For abused teens, drugs offer a means to escape. Sadly, some youth continue because they have become addicted.

Factual data adapted from information researched by Partnership for a Drug-Free America, The National Council on Alcoholism and Drug Dependence, and American Council for Drug Education.

Consider these statistics: Many teens are introduced to drugs by age 12 or 13. Marijuana is the most widely used illicit drug with 41 percent of all teens saying they have tried marijuana; 15.4 percent of 8th graders and 37 percent of 12th graders report past-year use. Nearly 25 percent of 8th graders report having been drunk at least once in their lives and nearly two-thirds of 12th graders; two-thirds of teens who drink report they can buy their own alcohol; the first use of alcohol typically begins around age 13; middle schoolers and high schoolers consume 1.1 billion cans of beer each year; 56 percent of students in grades 5-12 report that alcohol advertising encourages them to drink; alcohol-related automobile accidents are the leading cause of death among young people 15-24 years old; alcohol is the oldest and most widely used drug in the world.

While overall drug abuse is on the decline, these statistics tell us something about the willingness of our teens to experiment with harmful substances. Help your teens open the communication lines between parents, mentors, and yourself. The more they know—about the dangers and legalities—and the more welcome they feel to talk, the more likely they are to take a stand.

Theology and This Topic

Many Scripture references describe the body as God's dwelling place: "Do you not know that you are God's temple and that God's Spirit dwells in you? If anyone destroys God's temple, God will destroy that person. For God's temple is holy, and you are that temple" (1 Corinthians 3:16-17). Scripture admonishes persons who harm their bodies. If we believe that God gave us life and that God created us, we also must believe that to abuse what God gave us goes against the very gift of Creation. The use of drugs, including the abuse of alcohol and the use cigarettes, has been proven to tear down the body, not only physically but also emotionally and spiritually.

John Wesley regarded drunkenness as an evil. He believed to refrain from drinking was an intentional decision to "do no harm." Harm comes to the body and onto others when we abuse substances and do not exhibit self-control. Throughout the Epistles, Paul calls us to the opposite of abuse—self-control. The spirit is broken when it becomes dependent upon a thing or substance rather than the Source.

Read
John 15:19.

God grant me the serenity
to accept the things
I cannot change,
Courage to change
the things I can,
And the wisdom to know
the difference.
—Dr. Reinhold Niebuhr

You and the Scripture

Peer pressure is not particular to teenagers. Adults also experience peer pressure and find it difficult to resist the social pressures surrounding drinking, smoking, and drugs. Allow the words of John 15:19 to give you strength, purpose, and conviction. Ask God to give you discernment in sharing with your youth times you also experience peer pressure. Pray the "Serenity Prayer" in the margin.

Getting Hooked

Scripture: 1 Corinthians 3:16-17; 1 John 2:15-17; Luke 21:34

Take-Home Learning: Youth will learn that addictive behaviors can have long-term, even deadly, effects on our physical, emotional, and spiritual lives.

(key icon) indicates key activity. If time is limited, focus here.

activity	time	preparation	supplies
learning to stand			
(key) Take the Test! **AND** Debrief	5 minutes 10 minutes	Duplicate the True/False Fact Sheet (page 53). No preparation	True/False Fact Sheet, pens or pencils True/False Fact Sheet
Follow Me!	10 minutes	No preparation.	
strength to stand on			
(key) You Are a Temple!	10 minutes	No preparation	Bibles, student journals, pencils
standing room only			
(key) Practicing IBNO	5–10 minutes	Duplicate Just Don't Do It handout (page 54).	Just Don't Do It! handout
Great Comebacks! **AND** Debrief	10 minutes 5 minutes	Plan to have additional copies of True/False Fact Sheet (page 53).	Bibles, student journals, large sheet of paper, marker
standing on the promises			
Temptations The Challenge	10 minutes 5 minutes	No preparation No preparation	Bibles, student journals, pens or pencils Candles and matches

Learning to Stand

Provide the True/False Fact Sheet (page 53).

Note: Answers are printed at the bottom of the handout.

Leader's Guide

Take the Test! (5 minutes)

As youth arrive, give each one a copy of the True/False Fact Sheet (page 53) and direct them to begin taking the test! Allow the necessary time, but do not discuss the answers yet!

AND

Debrief (10 minutes)

If any youth arrived late, allow them a few minutes to complete the True/False Fact Sheet (page 53). Then call on volunteers to read aloud statements and their answers. If any youth give wrong answers, provide correct answers (see bottom of handout). Encourage them to write corrected answers on their handouts. Then ask:

- What information is new to you?
- Were you surprised by what you knew or didn't know?
- What is the most surprising mistake you made on the quiz?

Follow Me! (10 minutes)

As a way of introducing the topic of addictions, say: "Many teenagers use drugs, including alcohol and cigarettes, as a way to feel "free" and to help them relax, feel comfortable, or loosen up in social situations. They become addicted because they like the way the drugs make them feel, and their bodies become dependent on the chemicals that create those feelings. Their bodies then require more and more of the substances as the addictions worsen. Some teenagers begin using drugs because of peer pressure and do not realize the consequences of drug use."

Discuss with the youth the presence and availability of drugs in their schools and among their peers. Let them know that they should feel free to talk about the pressures they do or don't face to abuse drugs and alcohol.

Strength to Stand On

Provide Bibles, student journals, and pencils.

You Are a Temple! (10 minutes)

Have the youth work in pairs to read the Scriptures and answer the questions in their student journals (pages 20–21).

"You realize, don't you, that you are the temple of God, and God himself is present in you? No one will get by with vandalizing God's temple, you can be sure of that. God's temple is sacred—and you, remember, are the temple" (1 Corinthians 3:16-17, *Message*).

"Be on your guard. Don't let the sharp edge of your expectation get dulled by parties and drinking and shopping. Otherwise, that Day* is going to take you by complete surprise" (Luke 21:34, *Message*).

**The words "that Day" in this passage refer to the coming of the Son of Man, or the second coming. We are encouraged to watch and pray, not be doing other less meaningful things, so that we won't be caught by surprise.*

"Don't love the world's ways. Don't love the world's goods. Love of the world squeezes out love for the Father. Practically everything that goes on in the world—wanting your own way, wanting everything for yourself, wanting to appear important—has nothing to do with the Father. It just isolates you from him. The world and all its wanting, wanting, wanting, is on the way out—but whoever does what God wants is set for eternity" (1 John 2:15-17, *Message*).

Discuss the following questions:

- What do these Scriptures say about God?
- What do they say about human beings?
- What do they say about the relationship between God and human beings?
- How are we to understand what God would have us do about using drugs, drinking alcohol, and smoking?
- What have you learned from these Scriptures about peer pressure?

Practicing IBNO (5–10 minutes)

Standing Room Only

Provide Just Don't Do It handouts (page 54).

Duplicate Just Don't Do It handout.

Distribute the Just Don't Do It handouts (page 54) before asking a volunteer to read aloud the scenario. Then have the volunteer, or another youth, lead a discussion on using the IBNO steps to combat peer pressure. After the youth have discussed the scenario and the questions, ask:

- When have you faced a similar situation?
- Which character would you be in the story? Rob? Laney? One of the guys or girls? Not there at all?
- How can we avoid situations similar to this one?

Great Comebacks! (10 minutes)

Provide Bibles, student journals, a large sheet of paper, marker, True/False Fact Sheet (page 53), writing paper, and pens or pencils.

Plan to refer again to the True/False Fact Sheet.

Ask youth to brainstorm pressure lines they might hear from peers encouraging them to do drugs. Some examples are listed in their student journals (page 22). List responses on a large sheet of paper.

Divide the large group into smaller teams of two or three and assign several "pressure lines" to each group. Instruct each group to find a fact from the True/False Fact Sheet that relates to each pressure line and develop comebacks they might offer to those teens who pressure them. Encourage them to use the insights they gained from the Bible discussion. Consider the example on the next page:

Pressure Line: "Come on, a little bit won't hurt you."

Fact: More people die each year in the United States as a result of tobacco use than any other cause.

Comeback: "Don't you know the real reason why dragons are extinct? They smoked!"

AND

Debrief (5 minutes)

- How do statistics help us to overcome peer pressure?
- Does this information make you think twice about putting something harmful into your body? Why or why not?
- How can information, Scripture, rules from parents, and advice from youth workers combine to help you make good decisions?

Standing on the Promises

Temptations (10 minutes)

Provide Bibles, student journals, and pens or pencils.

Allow time for youth to write in their student journals. Direct them to answer the questions in the section "Temptations" (page 23). When they have finished writing, encourage them to continue thinking and praying about the questions. Invite them to talk to their parents or yourself about any information or thoughts presented in this session. Remind youth that an open conversation can lead to assurance in decision-making.

The Challenge (5 minutes)

Provide a candle and matches.

Ask youth to stand in a circle. Place a lighted candle in the center of the circle. Suggest youth spend closing moments sharing thoughts about ways they can warn their friends about the dangers of putting harmful substances into our bodies. After each individual shares, lead the large group to respond: "Lord, let me be a temple for you to live in." Close with a prayer for your youth and their struggles with peer pressure.

Session 6

Body Language

Topic: Appearance

Scripture: Romans 12:1-2; 1 Peter 3:4; 1 Samuel 16:7

Key Verse: "I appeal to you therefore, brothers and sisters, by the mercies of God, to present your bodies as a living sacrifice, holy and acceptable to God, which is your spiritual worship. Do not be conformed to this world, but be transformed by the renewing of your minds, so that you may discern what is the will of God—what is good and acceptable and perfect" (Romans 12:1-2).

Take-Home Learning: True beauty comes from being children of God, not from our outward appearances.

"What matters is not your outer appearance—the styling of your hair, the jewelry you wear, the cut of your clothes—but your inner disposition. Cultivate inner beauty, the gentle, gracious kind that God delights in" (1 Peter 3:3-4, *Message*).

Younger Youth and This Topic

The sameness that appears among cliques is a badge of membership. Look around any middle school or high school and you will observe groups of teenagers who are identically dressed. You'll see groups of preppies, jocks, goths, grunges, geeks, and skaters—to name a few. Belonging to one of these groups means wearing the "uniform."

Appearance is an expression of identity. Adolescents are trying on different identities in order to find the one that fits. Along the way, however, they can experience an enormous amount of stress to look "cool." In order to gain peer approval, youth experiment with everything from baggy clothes to skimpy clothes to makeup to wild hairstyles to diets to tattoos and body piercings.

Even as youth are trying out different looks, we can help them see their true beauty as being created in God's image. If they don't believe they possess real beauty, they are certain to look for beauty in outward things. Sometimes this search can cause harm to the body, and most times, the spirit.

Consider the problem of eating disorders during adolescence. Somehow we haven't communicated a sense of beauty and worth to those young people who think beauty equals thin. There are also dangers lurking for adolescent boys. While they may not be as prone to eating disorders, they do face the stress and pressure to grow big and tall—to be "strong"—which can result in the unhealthy use of steroids.

In recent years, tattoos and body piercings have become a trend among young people. In most states tattoos are illegal for minors, but no current regulations exist for body piercings (other than parental!). In some cases, these expressions fulfill a desire to be creative or to push the envelope. However, when these actions are explored to please other people or to fulfill a sense of worth, they become unhealthy. Teens need to understand the possible short- and long-term consequences and side effects of any permanent changes in body appearance. Most importantly, they need to know that they do not have to tattoo or pierce their bodies in order to belong.

As youth workers, help youth understand that their beauty does not come from the external "outfits" they may wear. Encourage them to look inside—and allow the Holy Spirit to fill their souls with a sense of beauty.

Theology and This Topic

God does not regard the way people dress or look. Rather, God always looks within to see the true condition and measure of a person's life. The Bible addresses our concerns over appearance. When our focus becomes pleasing others in our appearance, we lose our focus on pleasing God. As the passage in 1 Samuel teaches us, God looks at our heart. The Israelites had an image of what a king should look like—and David wasn't it! But God looked at David's heart and saw a man fit for a king. It's what's inside the heart that really matters.

Paul calls us to refrain from worrying about presenting our appearance outwardly and instead to present ourselves as a sacrifice to God in worship. Truly this applies today since we are pushed on every side to conform to a societal norm. As we are transformed by renewing our minds, we care more for what is pleasing and acceptable to God than what is defined as normal by our peers.

You and the Scripture

Read the key Scripture verse again. Think to yourself or journal about the ways in which you present your body as a holy sacrifice to God.

Can you recall the fads and trends during your adolescence? Most likely, your parents were as shocked and disapproving of your tastes and decisions as parents and leaders are of youth today. Remember also the rush of rebellion you felt when they told you their feelings about your tastes, decisions, friends, music, and so on. It's no different today. While we want to help teens express themselves in creative ways, we also want to help them affirm their inner beauty. I am reminded of three axioms told to me by my mother while growing up: "Beauty is in the eye of the beholder; Pretty is as pretty does; and Beauty is more than skin deep."

In your preparation for this session, pray for acceptance of your youth and understanding of their struggles for identity. Perhaps the prayer in the margin expresses your feelings.

**O Lord, teach me what I need to know.
Help me love all of your beautiful creation.
Let me praise you with my whole heart.
Make me cling to what you love and turn away from what you hate.
Teach me to let you be the judge and to please you by giving you my life.**

—based on a prayer by Thomas 'a Kempis

Body Language

Scripture: Romans 12:1-2; 1 Peter 3:4; 1 Samuel 16:7

Take-Home Learning: True beauty comes from being children of God, not from our outward appearances.

indicates key activity. If time is limited, focus here.

activity	time	preparation	supplies
learning to stand			
What's In? What's Out?	5 minutes	Collect a variety of fashion catalogs and teen magazines.	Magazines, large sheet of paper, glue, scissors
and			
Who Do You Say I Am?	10 minutes	No preparation	No supplies
strength to stand on			
Beauty Is More Than Skin Deep	10 minutes	Prepare a paraphrase of one of the Scripture passages on page 40.	Bibles, *The Message* or other modern translation, large sheet of paper, marker, paper and pencils
"I Say/You Say"	20–25 minutes	Duplicate Body Piercing/Tattoo Information Sheet (page 55).	Body Piercing/Tattoo Information Sheet, pencils
standing room only			
Practicing IBNO	5–10 minutes	Duplicate additional copies of IBNO handout (page 49) if needed.	IBNO handout
standing on the promises			
What I Like About Me! The Challenge	5 minutes 5 minutes	Obtain a CD player and a selection of background music. No preparation	Bibles, student journals, pencils, CD player, CDs Candles and matches

Learning to Stand

Provide posterboard or a large sheet of paper, glue, scissors, teen magazines, and fashion catalogs to create collages.

Strength to Stand On

Provide Bibles (The Message or other modern translations), student journals, a large sheet of paper, marker, writing paper, and pencils.

Prepare your own personal paraphrase for one of the Scripture passages.

**This passage of Scripture is a set of instructions for women in the community of faith, but the essence of the message can help us think about appearance. Our lives are to be exemplary because of our faith, not our looks. This passage calls us to inward virtue that is not swayed by how others tell us we ought to look or act.*

What's In? What's Out? (5 minutes)

As youth arrive, invite them to design the perfect "cool" look using pictures from magazines and catalogs. Encourage them to choose clothing, accessories, haircuts, shoes, jewelry, and so on by cutting and pasting the different pictures. Then ask them to design an "uncool" look.

AND

Who Do You Say I Am? (10 minutes)

Ask for volunteers to explain their "cool" outfits using the following questions:

- What makes this look cool to you?
- What does this look say about you?
- Would you actually wear these clothes?
- Who determines that this look is cool? Does it matter what your friends think? For whom do you dress?

When all youth have shared, ask them to explain their "uncool" outfits using the following questions:

- What does this look say about the person who wears it?
- Would you hang out with someone who dresses like this?

Beauty Is More Than Skin Deep (10 minutes)

Have three youth read aloud one of the following Scripture passages using a modern translation such as *The Message or CEV*: Romans 12:3, 1 Peter 3:4*, and 1 Samuel 16:7. Ask each youth to choose a passage and paraphrase it. The idea is to motivate youth to think carefully about the meanings and values of various words. Share your personal paraphrase as an example. After five minutes, invite volunteers to read aloud their paraphrases.

After a few minutes, ask the entire group to compose one sentence summarizing the central idea of all three passages. Write the sentence on a large sheet of paper. (*For example, "Beauty is more than skin deep."*)

Ask:

- What is beauty?
- In what ways do we try to change ourselves to become more "beautiful"?
- What could we do to think of ourselves as beautiful without adding, taking away from, or changing anything about ourselves?

• How can our bodies be holy and living sacrifices to God?

Take a few moments for youth to work individually to read and paraphrase the Scriptures on pages 24–25 in the student journal.

"I Say/You Say" (15–20 minutes)

Provide Body Piercing/Tattoo Information Sheet (page 55) and pencils.

Duplicate Body Piercing/Tattoo Information Sheet.

Talk together about today's body piercing/tattoo trends, then organize a debate. Assign youth to four different research teams. Pass out the Body Piercing/Tattoo Information Sheets (page 55) and assign one question to each group.

- Group 1: Why is it OK to have a tattoo?
- Group 2: Why is it dangerous or risky to have a tattoo?
- Group 3: Why is it OK to have a body piercing?
- Group 4: Why is body piercing dangerous or risky?

Allow approximately five minutes for groups to prepare their arguments. Direct each group to prepare three brief arguments related to the assigned question. Encourage groups to include information from the handout, the Bible study, and their personal opinions.

Call for groups one and two to present their arguments one at a time. Allow five minutes for each group. Then call for groups three and four to begin their arguments one at a time. Again, allow five minutes for each group.

When all four arguments have been presented, say: "Body piercing and tattoos can have harmful effects on the body, and tattoos should be considered permanent. Tattoo-removal surgery is very painful and expensive! Some people consider tattoos and body piercings an art form, but others believe the harm and risk to the body is too great. While beauty can be seen on the outside, our Scripture lessons teach that beauty comes from being children of God—from the inside—who we are at our core. Sure, some of us wear makeup and worry about our hairstyles and want to wear nice clothes, but that doesn't determine our beauty."

Practicing IBNO (5–10 minutes)

Standing Room Only

Provide additional copies of IBNO handout (page 49) if necessary.

Say something like: "You might not confront outright peer pressure to look a certain way. I mean your friends probably aren't hounding you to get a tattoo, belly ring, or a certain outfit. But you probably hear subtle hints through the media and are influenced by how your brain responds when your best friend says he or she thinks something is "cool." We want to be liked and accepted, so when somebody tells us what they think is cool, it's easy for us to assume it's true.

"If our friends continually offer us putdowns or make fun of the way we look, we should probably evaluate the sincerity of the friendship. It's hard enough feeling good about ourselves; we don't need other people telling us how we should feel. Sometimes we can become so worried about our appearances that we get depressed, develop eating disorders, or become anxious and stressed. Let's talk about how IBNO can help us deal with pressure to look a certain way." Review and discuss the following:

- Investigate the messages. Be informed. What subtle messages do we receive from the media, friends, and our subconscious?
- Be smart. If you change the way you look by getting a tattoo, body piercing, or some other trend, will you get in trouble? Are you respecting yourself? Are you breaking the law by getting a tattoo? What are possible consequences?
- Know how to respond and it's no problem! What do you say when you're told you need to look or act a certain way? How do you respond when you hear messages that you need to lose weight, bulk up, or spend all your money on that one perfect outfit?
- Remember that you are the beautiful creation of a Beautiful Creator. You can overcome the pressure because you can do all things in Christ who calls you to live in the world but not be of it. How are you living as a faithful follower of Jesus Christ?

Standing on the Promises

Provide Bibles, student journals, pencils, a cassette or CD for background music, and a CD player.

Consider playing soft music while the youth journal.

Provide a candle and matches.

What I Like About Me! (5 minutes)

Allow time for youth to write in their student journals using pages 25–26, listing qualities or characteristics they like about themselves.

The Challenge (5 minutes)

Ask youth to stand in a circle and place a lighted candle in the center. Encourage youth to share ways they will respond during the week to friends who talk about their peers in a negative way because of their appearance. After each youth shares, ask the group to respond by saying: "Lord, help us to see beauty in all people." Close with the prayer on page 27 in the student journal:

Beautiful God, thank you for taking good care of me. Help me to find my beauty in you. Forgive me for worrying about my outward appearance. I know that you see inside to the real me. Let me be transformed and know your will. May my life be pleasing and acceptable in your sight. In Jesus' name, Amen.

Session 7

Standing Among Friends

Topic: Positive Peer Pressure

Scripture: Hebrews 10:24-25; Romans 15:5-6

Key Verse: "And let us consider how to provoke one another to love and good deeds, not neglecting to meet together, as is the habit of some, but encouraging one another, and all the more as you see the Day approaching" (Hebrews 10:24-25).

Take-Home Learning: Surrounding ourselves with good, Christian friends makes dealing with peer pressure easier.

Younger Youth and This Topic

We have spent the last six sessions looking at the role of negative peer pressure and how the Bible helps us respond to that pressure. Now let's turn our thoughts to the influence of positive peer pressure. Session two identified ways peer pressure can influence people to change their minds from what they know to be a correct answer to an incorrect answer—just because everyone else gives the incorrect answer! But the opposite is true as well. It only takes one person to stand up and tell the truth, and others will feel free to say what's right, too. These results confirm the need in adolescents to be accepted, to belong, and to stand with their peers. The results also reveal the importance of helping our youth choose some good friends to travel with them on the Christian journey.

Peer pressure *can be* positive. The peer group *can* be a source of affection, sympathy, courage, and understanding. It is a place for experimentation and a supportive setting for achieving the two primary developmental tasks of adolescence: (1) identity—finding the answer to the question "Who am I?" and (2) autonomy—discovering self as separate and independent from parents.

Two of our tasks as youth leaders are to help our teenagers develop a healthy awareness of self so that they feel like valued individuals and to nurture our teenagers' abilities so they can build positive peer relationships.

"Let's see how inventive we can be in encouraging love and helping out, not avoiding worshiping together as some do but spurring each other on" (Hebrews 10:24-25, *Message*).

Theology and This Topic

The church is called to be a nurturing environment. In the early church, communities were described with these words: "See how they love each other." Jesus gathered a small group of twelve to share in his mission of love on this earth. They were his peers, and they were a group whose purpose was to build up one another and to be extensions of Christ to the world. Jesus never sent them out individually. He sent them two by two so that they could strengthen each other and share each other's burdens. In our churches today, we form small groups with common interests for support and mission. Often those small groups are made up of those with like mind and belief systems; they are peer groups. Jesus said, "Where two or three are gathered in my name, I am there among them" (Matthew 18:20). In recent years, there has been a resurgence of the small-group model. Many small groups take on a structure much like our youth's peer groups.

You and the Scripture

Read **Hebrews 10:24-25.**

Reread the key verse for today from *The Message* (printed in the margin on page 43). Think about how your friends support you in your Christian journey.

As faith communities, we are called to build up one another and encourage, even "provoke," love in everyone. As you prepare to teach this final session on peer pressure, consider how you will provoke love in your youth. How will you encourage them to be positive influences in their peer groups and share the love of Christ even when they're pressured in all directions?

Pray for your youth that they might associate with peer groups who support them, love them, and encourage them to be all that they can be in Christ.

Standing Among Friends

Scripture: Hebrews 10:24-25; Romans 15:5-6

Take-Home Learning: Surrounding ourselves with good, Christian friends makes dealing with peer pressure easier.

indicates key activity. If time is limited, focus here.

activity	time	preparation	supplies
learning to stand			
A Good Friend Is . . .	5 minutes	No preparation	Writing paper and pencils
or			
Human Knots	10 minutes	Review activity instructions on page 46.	No supplies
strength to stand on			
With Like Minds	10 minutes	Write Bible passages on a large sheet of paper and post in meeting room.	Bibles, student journals, pencils, large sheet of paper, marker
standing room only			
Who Are My Friends?	15 minutes	No preparation	Bibles, student journals, pencils
Practicing IBNO	5-10 minutes	Duplicate additional copies of IBNO handout (page 49).	IBNO handout
standing on the promises			
What Are Friends For? The Challenge	10 minutes	Choose a song related to friends for background music. No preparation	CD player, background music, Bibles, student journals, pencils Candle and matches

Learning to Stand

Provide writing paper and pencils.

A Good Friend Is ... (5 minutes)

As youth arrive, give each a piece of paper and a pencil. Ask them to describe what they believe is a good friend.

OR

Human Knots (10 minutes)

Help youth to understand the concept of working together to resolve a situation—or to get themselves out of a "knot." The activity emphasizes how peer groups can help us to resist peer pressure.

Create the knot by gathering in a circle, shoulders touching, and stretching your hands toward the center of the circle. Tell everyone to grab a couple of hands. Make sure that no one is holding only one persons' hands or the hands of the person standing next to him or her. Then instruct youth to work together to untie their human knot.

Say: "Since you are all tangled in the same knot, you must agree on some method to 'untangle.'" When you have successfully unravelled the knot, hopefully your group will be standing in one large circle. Play the game again if time permits.[2]

[2]Adapted from *The New Games Book*, edited by Andrew Fluegelman (Headlands Press, Inc., 1976); page 69.

Ask:

- What does this game teach us about peer groups and peer pressure?
- How does working together to solve a problem make the problem easier to solve?

Strength to Stand On

Provide Bibles, student journals, pens or pencils, large sheet of paper, and marker.

Write the Bible passages on a large sheet of paper and post in the meeting room.

With Like Minds (10 minutes)

Say: "The Scripture lessons for today teach us how to be good friends and how we should be in community with one another. I'd like for you to work in groups of two to three, read the Scriptures printed in your student journals, and answer the questions in the section "With Like Minds" (page 28).

"Let's see how inventive we can be in encouraging love and helping out, not avoiding worshiping together as some do but spurring each other on" (Hebrews 10:24-25, *Message*).

"May our dependably steady and warmly personal God develop maturity in you so that you get along with each other as well as Jesus gets along with us all. Then we'll be a choir—not our voices only, but our very lives singing in harmony in a stunning anthem to the God and Father of our Master Jesus!" (Romans 15:5-6, *Message*).

After the small groups have spent some time discussing the questions, call the youth back together and discuss any insights they might have gained. Then, ask the questions again:

- What do you think the writers (who were inspired by God) intended to say to those for whom the passages were written?
- What do these passages have to say to us today about peer groups?
- If you took these passages seriously, what changes would you make in your life?
- How does your faith help you to be a better friend?

Who Are My Friends? (15 minutes)

Say, "Now we're going to evaluate the support system we have in our friends. We described earlier what we believe a good friend to be. Let's see if that matches up with the friends we have now."

Refer youth to "Who Are My Friends?" on page 29 in the student journal. Instruct youth to list the positive qualities their good friends possess and then write a few words about any areas in which they feel torn down by their friends. Use the questions as talkpoints and encourage the students to write in their student journals.

Say: "Good friends can help us overcome the stress we receive in the form of peer pressure. When we surround ourselves with people who respect our beliefs and can help us be faithful in our relationships with God, then we are more likely to take a stand in times of trouble."

Standing Room Only

Provide Bibles, student journals, and pencils.

Refer to the descriptions of friends they wrote in the opening activity.

Practicing IBNO (5–10 minutes)

Distribute the IN BUT NOT OF handouts again (page 49) and lead a discussion of how these steps can help you become a positive peer pressure among your friends.

Ask:

- How can you help a friend identify that he or she is being pressured?
- How can you and your friends help one another to see the beauty inside one another?
- How can you speak the truth when others are lying?
- How can your knowledge of Scripture help you overcome negative peer pressure?
- What does it mean to be "in" and not "of" the world?

Provide the IN BUT NOT OF handout (page 49).

Playing Friends (5–8 minutes)

Lead the group to develop a scenario demonstrating positive peer pressure. Then direct them to write an open-ended skit using the scenario. When the skit is finished, ask the group to perform the skit with a positive ending. Act out the skit several times, choosing a different volunteer(s) and performing a different ending each time. See how many positive endings the group can act out.

After several skit endings have been performed, talk about ways they can be a positive peer pressure in real situations they encounter.

Standing on the Promises

Provide student journals, pens or pencils, and Bibles.

Choose a song about friendship to play as background music.

What Are Friends For? (10 Minutes)

Play a song that talks about standing together while youth complete the questions in "What Are Friends For?" (page 30) in their student journals.

Provide a candle and matches.

The Challenge (5 minutes)

Ask youth to stand in a circle and place a lighted candle in the middle of the circle. Encourage youth to spend the closing moments sharing some ways they can be good friends and be positive influences in their peer groups. After each youth contributes, lead the group to say: "Lord, help me choose true friendship." Close with a prayer for your youth.

Session One Reproducible Page

IN BUT NOT OF

I have told you these things, so that in me you may have peace. In this world you will have trouble. But take heart! I have overcome the world" (John 16:33, NIV).

OK. So you've got a great set of friends who would never pressure you into doing something or going somewhere you don't feel you should go, right? They're such great friends that you have decided to band together to stand up to the pressure situations you find yourselves in. Even so, sometime in your own life you'll run smack into the inevitable—peer pressure. So how can we be "in" the crowd without being "of" the crowd? How can we enjoy the maximum number of friends, love our neighbors, but still say "no" when we need to? Remember—IN BUT NOT OF or IBNO. That is, try these four no-brainer steps when it comes to peer pressure!

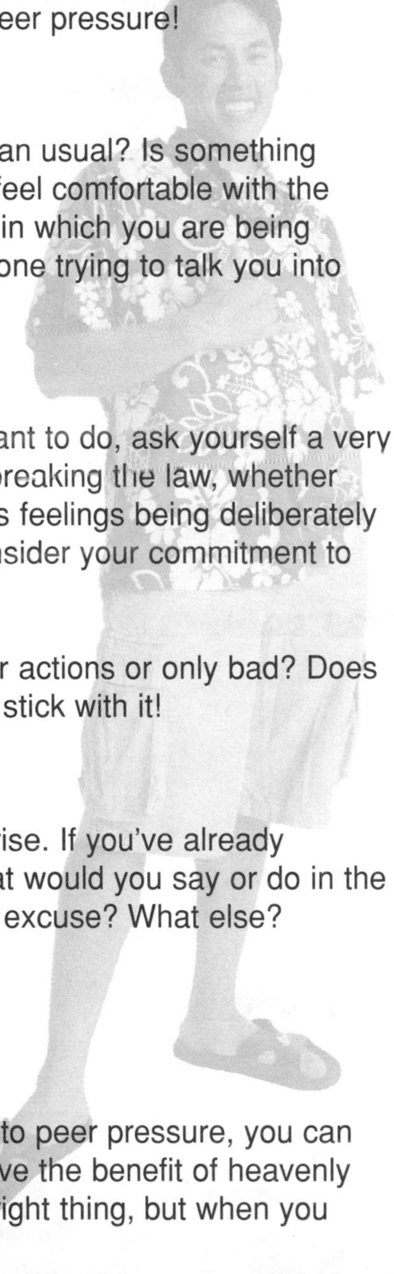

INVESTIGATE THE SITUATION

Be aware of your surroundings. Are your friends acting differently than usual? Is something "up"? Do you have a chaperone? Would your parents or guardians feel comfortable with the situation? Really listen to the conversation around you and the way in which you are being spoken to. Do you feel pressure to make a quick decision? Is someone trying to talk you into something?

BE SMART

If you feel like you're being persuaded to do something you don't want to do, ask yourself a very basic question—"Will I get in trouble?" Think about whether you're breaking the law, whether your parents or whoever is in authority will be upset? Are someone's feelings being deliberately hurt or is someone intentionally being disrespected? And finally, consider your commitment to God—does the situation compromise your faithfulness to God?

Consider the consequences. Could something good come from your actions or only bad? Does one outweigh the other? Is it worth it? Commit to your decision and stick with it!

NO PROBLEM

Know what you will say and do in pressure situations before they arise. If you've already planned how to respond, then the pressure will be no problem! What would you say or do in the face of peer pressure? Would you say no? go home? have a ready excuse? What else?

OVERCOME

Because you have thought ahead and feel empowered to stand up to peer pressure, you can feel confident and sweat-free. With Jesus Christ on our side, we have the benefit of heavenly power to overcome. Of course, sometimes it will be hard to do the right thing, but when you have a plan in place, you're more likely to succeed! You can do it!

Session Two Reproducible Page

Making a Difference

Instructions: Finish the story using IBNO.

Maria is in the "in" crowd and might be considered the most popular girl in school. Her clique is a mix of boys and girls. One Friday night, Maria hosts a party in her basement. While everyone in her class was invited, the "in" crowd seems to be having all the fun. Ryan and Chris notice that some guys are hanging out by the stairs. They go over and begin making fun of them and asking the guys why they even bothered to come to their party. Maria notices the situation and she …

Investigate the Situation

Be Smart

No Problem

Overcome

Session Three Reproducible Page

FEELING THE PRESSURE

SITUATION ONE:

You and a friend are walking home from school and stop to get a soda at the convenience store. Together you have only enough money to buy two cans of pop. You see your friend pick up a bag of chips and stuff it inside her jacket. She looks at you and says: "Here take one too. I do it all the time. Nobody will know; they can't see us."

SITUATION TWO:

Your best friend asks to see your homework. You think it's OK and give it to her. She quickly copies it and together you walk to class. The teacher passes out a surprise pop quiz on the very homework subject you just turned in. Your friend gets your attention and says she needs to copy off of your paper. If she doesn't, the teacher will know that she has cheated and may suspect you too.

SITUATION THREE:

Your friends are going to a concert. They bought a ticket for you because, without asking your parents first, you said you would go. When you did ask your parents, they said no. They believed the concert was not one you should attend. Your friend's mother offered to call your parents and invite you to spend the night. Now you could attend the concert, and your parents would never know. After all, your friends bought the ticket because you said you would go!

FAMOUS PEER PRESSURE LINES

- "You won't let your friends down, will you?"
- "It's no big deal. Everybody is doing it."
- "We won't get caught. Come on, it will be fun."
- "Trust me. No one will find out."
- "I dare you."
- "What are you—a chicken?"
- "What a goody-goody! You're no fun!"
- "Be cool!"
- "I thought you were my friend. If you were, you'd do this with me."
- "Don't be stupid."
- "Grow up!"
- "If you do this for me, I'll give you ________."
- "If you don't take risks, you can't be my friend."

Session Four Reproducible Page

Party Time

Fourteen-year-old Cindy invited four of her closest friends to her house for a slumber party to celebrate her birthday. She also invited her boyfriend Chris, who is 16, and four of his friends. When her friends arrived, Chris and his friends were already there. What Cindy did not tell her friends was that her parents were away for the weekend. Her parents left home thinking that she was spending the weekend with her best friend Kaitlyn. Initially, Kaitlyn was very upset with Cindy. She was afraid that her parents would find out, and she knew they would not approve of her being at any friend's house without the parents being present. They also would not allow her to be there while boys were there. It was against the house rules they had agreed on. Kaitlyn thought about calling her parents to come and get her, but Cindy quickly convinced her that everything would be OK. Cindy knew she would get into even more trouble, because her parents thought she was staying at Kaitlyn's for the weekend. Cindy called Kaitlyn a prude and reminded her that she had arranged for a guy she really liked to be at the party.

Quickly it became very clear that each girl had been paired with an older boy. Kaitlyn had been paired with Steve, the guy she had often admired in school. They had fun dancing and playing games. At first the party seemed to be harmless until Cindy and her boyfriend Chris left the room and went upstairs. Eventually, the other three girls and boys seemed to drift off to other parts of the house. Soon Kaitlyn and Steve were alone. Steve began kissing her and telling her that he had noticed her in school and thought that she was very pretty. Kaitlyn was very flattered and decided that kissing was OK. She had not had any experiences in kissing thus far, and this felt good. After awhile, Steve began trying to take off her clothes. When he sensed her reluctance, he told her that she was very hot and really turned him on. When Kaitlyn strongly resisted, he asked her if she wanted to embarrass herself with her friends? She was so scared that she said nothing more while he had sex with her. She was hurt and humiliated.

The next day when Kaitlyn's mother picked her up from Cindy's house, she noticed Kaitlyn had been crying. When they reached home, her mother asked her why she had been crying. Worried that she might be pregnant, Kaitlyn told her mother what had happened at Cindy's party. Her mother wanted to call the police, but Kaitlyn was afraid of more humiliation. Instead, her mother scheduled her a doctor's appointment.

The good news was that Kaitlyn was not pregnant. But she had contracted genital warts from Steve, and she was going to take an AIDS test to be sure that he had not given her that deadly disease as well. Even more bad news was that Steve had told the whole school about being with Kaitlyn.

Session Five Reproducible Page

TRUE/FALSE FACT SHEET

Circle true or false for each question.

1. **TRUE OR FALSE**: Alcohol is a stimulant. It speeds up the body's processes.
2. **TRUE OR FALSE:** Alcohol is the most abused drug in the world.
3. **TRUE OR FALSE:** The average age for people to start drinking in the United States is fifteen years.
4. **TRUE OR FALSE:** During a weekend, an average of one teenager (age 15-20) dies each hour in a car crash—nearly 50 percent involve alcohol.
5. **TRUE OR FALSE:** Nearly two-thirds of high school seniors have been drunk in their lifetimes.
6. **TRUE OR FALSE:** One in 4 eighth graders have been drunk in their lifetimes.
7. **TRUE OR FALSE:** Almost half of all high school seniors have used illicit drugs in their lifetime.
8. **TRUE OR FALSE:** More than 4 out of 5 eighth graders have not used drugs in the past month.
9. **TRUE OR FALSE:** The tobacco industry earns less than one billion dollars a year from the illegal sale of tobacco to children.
10. **TRUE OR FALSE:** Fifty percent of all eighth graders have tried cigarettes.
11. **TRUE OR FALSE:** The average age of first tobacco use in the United States is 18.
12. **TRUE OR FALSE:** More people die each year in the United States as a result of tobacco use than any other cause.
13. **TRUE OR FALSE:** Tobacco use will discolor your teeth, wrinkle the skin on your face, and may cause oral cancer.
14. **TRUE OR FALSE:** Teens are more likely to be influenced to smoke by advertising than peer pressure.
15. **TRUE OR FALSE:** While alcohol stays in the system 24 hours, marijuana only stays in the system for 8 hours.
16. **TRUE OR FALSE:** Marijuana users feel thirsty, but have no appetite.
17. **TRUE OR FALSE:** More than 25 percent of high school seniors are current marijuana users.
18. **TRUE OR FALSE:** Some short-term effects of marijuana use are problems with memory and learning, loss of coordination, increased heart rate, clear thinking, and problem-solving.

Information adapted from: Monitoring the Future; Partnership for a Drug-Free America; National Institute on Drug Abuse; Mothers Against Drunk Driving; American Council for Drug Education; Campaign for Tobacco-Free Kids; National Center for Tobacco-Free Kids.

Answers: 1–False: Alcohol is a depressant and slows down the body's functions; 2–True; 3–False: The average age at which teens begin to drink is almost 13; 4–True; 5–True; 6–True; 7–True; 8–True; 9–False: The tobacco industry earns more than 1.5 billion dollars from the sale of tobacco to children; 10–True; 11–False: The average age at which teens begin using tobacco is a little more than 12; 12–True; 13–True; 14–True; 15–False: Marijuana can stay in the body up to one month; 16–False: Marijuana users have a huge appetite sometimes referred to as the "munchies"; 17–False: Fewer than one in four high school seniors is a current marijuana user; 18–True.

Session Five Reproducible Page

Just Don't Do It!

Rob has just gotten the inside information on a rave party happening this weekend. He has had a rough week and is ready to blow off some steam. Luckily, his parents are out of town, so he doesn't have to worry about curfew. All of his friends are coming over early on Friday night to get the party started before heading to the rave. Some guys head straight for the garage to inhale; others have started working on the beer in the fridge. They are passing time till the girls arrive, then they'll head to the party.

Laney is excited about her first rave party because she loves to dance. But she's nervous about the amount of drugs and alcohol she's heard is available at these parties. All of her friends have "raved," so Laney wants to fit in. But she really doesn't want to drink or take drugs. She hasn't told her mom she's going to the rave, but she feels confident that she won't compromise her values. The girls are ready and head over to Rob's.

When the whole gang makes it to the rave, the guys are drunk and the girls are trying to score some ecstasy. Laney only wants to dance. Her friends find some ecstasy and are really pressuring Laney to try it. Laney just keeps dancing since she has made some new friends on the dance floor. Her friends give up on getting Laney to take the ecstasy willingly and slip it into her soft drink. Before Laney knows what hit her, the group is dancing crazy and she feels totally out of control. Unlike her friends, who seem to be having a great time, Laney is scared and doesn't know what to do.

What can Laney do at this point in the night?

What could she have done differently?

Does Laney have good friends? Why or why not?

Do you think they even considered the fact that they were breaking the law? How good an argument against drinking and abusing drugs is the fact that it is illegal?

Laney had good intentions for the night. She was certain that she wasn't going to do anything wrong. However, something totally out of her control occurred and she ended up scared and unable to react with her full presence of mind. How could IBNO help Laney make better decisions in the future?

Luckily the gang made it home safely except for the number of brain cells they killed. What are some possible dangers that could have happened to any of them?

Session Six Reproducible Page

BODY PIERCING/TATTOOS INFORMATION SHEET

Tattoos are cool!
- Over the past few years, tattoos have grown in acceptance by society.
- Tattoos are considered an accepted art form. In fact, the tattoo art has been shown in galleries around the world, and the prices have skyrocketed.
- Tattoos can be a means of personal expression.
- From 4000–2000 B.C., Egyptians wore tattoos as a means to identify fertility and nobility.
- Lady Randolph Churchill (Winston's mother) had a snake tattooed around her wrist.
- Tattoos may be an expression of belonging.

Tattoos are not cool!
- In our time, tattoos have been associated with identifying specific groups. Bikers often wear tattoos to identify themselves to a particular biker group, and many gangs wear the same tattoos to express loyalty to that gang.
- Tattoo equipment and needles that are not sterile can spread serious infections: hepatitis, tetanus, or possibly HIV.
- Tattoos, which cost approximately fifty dollars to apply, may cost more than one thousand dollars to remove.
- Tattoos are difficult and painful to remove and may cause permanent discoloration.
- Some people's bodies are allergic to tattoo dye and reject the tattoo.
- A person cannot donate blood for one year after getting a tattoo.
- You do not have to wear a tattoo to belong.

Body piercing is cool!
- Body piercing may express belonging to a specific group.
- In the past, body piercing often identified royalty and signified courage and virility.
- The Mayans pierced their tongues as a spiritual ritual.
- Body piercing often is a means of personal expression.

Body piercing is not cool!
- You do not need piercing to belong.
- Blood donations are not accepted for one year after a body piercing.
- Unsterile body-piercing instruments can lead to infections from bacteria, blood poisoning, and viruses.
- After a piercing, experts say that complete healing varies from several months to as much as two years.
- Since body piercing can be expensive, many youth attempt to pierce themselves.
- Healing time can depend on a variety of factors: health, weight, diet, clothes, and aftercare.

A Retreat: The Pressure Is On!

Purpose: To help youth overcome negative peer pressure and become positive Christian influences among their friends.

Preparation

Several weeks before the retreat, form small groups of both adults and youth to plan and implement the retreat. Plan for a weekend retreat to be held in your local church or in a camp or retreat center. Choose one youth and one adult to co-direct the retreat and coordinate small-group planning. Find and reserve the retreat location. The facility should have electricity for viewing movies and listening to music. Also, choose a location that is accessible to a shopping mall.

Determine cost per person for the retreat. Provide registration and permission forms, and set a registration deadline. Send a letter to parents detailing retreat plans and activities. Inform them you will be discussing sensitive issues such as sex and drugs.

Determine rules for communal living (cleaning and cooking, if applicable) and clean-up chores, sleeping arrangements, and so forth. Provide a student journal for each participant and remind youth to bring their Bibles.

If you have a large group of youth, divide the group into "cliques" of eight to ten for small-group work and Bible study time. Assign the small groups names of popular cliques in their schools—jocks, loners, skaters, and so on.

Sample Schedule

Friday

Settling In	**5:00**
Welcome Introductions	**5:30**
Dinner	**6:00**
Bible Study	**7:00**

Friday

Allow time for youth to locate their rooms/dorms and settle in. When teens have reassembled, introduce adult retreat leaders and explain the retreat theme. Welcome any visiting youth before reviewing conduct rules and walking through the schedule. Give any instructions concerning dinner.

Before beginning Bible study, play a few ice-breaker games and sing some silly camp songs. Also sing some familiar praise songs to transition to Bible study. Read together Luke 9:25 and Proverbs 13:20. Discuss the following questions:

- What do these passages mean to you?
- Is popularity very important to you?
- What kind of popularity would make you happy?
- What kids are popular at school? Would you want to be like them if you could?

- What would you have to change about yourself to make that happen? What would Jesus say about that change?

Read aloud Matthew 19:19b and ask the following questions:

- Would you say that you generally feel good about yourself? Why?
- Is there anything you'd like to change about yourself? Anything you might be willing to share with the group?
- True or False: If you don't love yourself, it's impossible to love others.

7:30 What Is Peer Pressure?

What Is Peer Pressure?

Have youth break into their small groups and write a definition of the term *peer pressure.* When they have completed their final definitions, ask them to write them on pieces of paper and display in your meeting space. Invite each group to explain its definition. Ask all the groups:

- How does peer pressure affect you based on these definitions?

- What experiences of dealing with peer pressure might you be willing to share?

Say, "This weekend we are going to talk about the negative aspects of peer pressure, but more importantly, we will discover that Christ calls us to be positive peer pressure in tough situations."

8:00 Movie Time

9:45 Movie Discussion

Show the movie, *A Walk to Remember.* Discuss the scenes that illustrate peer pressure and talk about the main character's willingness to be herself and not give in to the pressures. (For a discussion guide and activities for *A Walk to Remember,* visit *ileadyouth.com/reeltoreal.asp.*)

10:00 Snack/Music

10:30 Evening Devotion

What Makes You Different ... Makes You Beautiful (Evening Devotion)

To begin the evening devotion, ask the following:

- Is it OK to be different?
- How am I different?
- Am I afraid to be myself with my friends?

Distribute writing paper and pencils to youth. Instruct them to write a prayer to God, asking for courage to be themselves. After a few minutes, ask if any are willing to share their prayers with the group.

Now instruct youth to tear small slips of paper from the bottom of their letters and write the following words: "I'm good enough for God; so I'm good enough for ________________________." Instruct youth to write their names in the blanks and to carry the papers in their pockets this weekend, so that each time they put their hands in their pockets, they will be reminded that they are good enough for God and themselves.

10:45 Game time

11:00 Go to Rooms

12:00 Lights Out

Play a game before calling it a night!

Saturday

7:00 Wake up

8:00 Breakfast

8:30 Clean up

9:00 Morning Devotion

Saturday

What I Like About Me! (Morning Devotion)

Ask for volunteers to read aloud the following Scriptures using *The Message* or a modern translation: Romans 12:1-2; 1 Peter 3:4; and 1 Samuel 16:7.

Say: "God made us with great skill and crafted us with loving care. How do you understand our value as creations of God?"

Ask youth to turn to "What I Like About Me!" in the student journal (pages 25–26) and complete the activity.

- What do you see when you look in the mirror?
- List words you use to describe yourself.
- Describe a time when you felt really good about yourself.
- How would your friends describe you?
- How would you describe yourself?
- If you were to describe the music of your soul, what would it sound like? A rock song? A hymn? A slow love song? A praise song?

In conclusion, read aloud the following Scripture. Jesus said: "Therefore I tell you, do not worry about your life, what you will eat or what you will drink, or about your body, what you will wear. … Are you not of more value than they?" (Matthew 6:25, 26).

9:30 Bible Study

To begin the Bible study time, read aloud Romans 12:9-10, Philippians 4:13, and 1 Timothy 4:12. Ask and discuss the following questions:

- What is each passage saying about the identity of a Christian?

  A Christian is …

- What does this passage have to say about being a positive role model?
- How do I become a force for positive peer pressure?
- What changes do I need to make in my life to participate in positive peer pressure?
- Where can I receive the courage to make those changes?

10:00 Identifying Peer Pressure

12:00 Lunch
Free time

2:00 Field Trip

Practicing IBNO

If possible, schedule an outing to the local shopping mall. Break into groups of two or three to look for peer pressure situations that may be occurring. Encourage youth to consider these questions while at the mall: Is anyone being bullied? Is a group of friends hanging out in the food court? What's happening there? Do you feel pressured to buy something trendy? How could negative peer pressure happen here? What about positive peer pressure?

Distribute the IN BUT NOT OF handout (page 49) and have a youth-led discussion about ways these steps might help them overcome negative peer pressure and equip them to have a positive influence on their peers.

Saturday Evening

Making a Difference

Divide youth into their small groups and give them the Making a Difference handout on page 50. Direct them to read the scenario and fill in the remainder of the story. Once they have completed the story using the IBNO steps, instruct each group to create a skit based on the new scenarios. Allow adequate time to rehearse and then introduce groups to perform their skits. Vote to see who wins the "Oscar" for best writing and acting. Award a silly prize.

Standing on the Promises (Evening Devotion)

Read aloud John 15:12-16. Say, "Jesus defines true friends as those willing to lay down their lives for their friends." Ask:

- What does it mean to be humble?
- Do you have trouble accepting people as they are?
- Are you a good friend?

Ask youth to use their student journals (page 6) to write about a time when they helped someone else and it made them feel good.

After a few minutes say, "Ralph Waldo Emerson said, 'The only way to have a friend is to be one.'" Ask: "What does this statement mean? What are you willing to give to your friends?" Close in a prayer for friends.

Play some more late-night games or have a board-game tournament.

Sunday

A Good Friend Is ... (Morning Devotion)

Display sheets of large paper or posterboard with the words "A Good Friend Is ..." written at the tops. Ask youth to think about what a good friend is and write their ideas on the posters.

Read aloud the following verses:

"May our dependably steady and warmly personal God develop maturity in you so that you get along with each other as well as Jesus gets along with us all. Then we'll be a choir—not our voices only, but our very lives singing in harmony in a stunning anthem to the God and Father of our Master Jesus!" (Romans 15:5-6, *Message*)

Saturday Evening

5:00	Dinner Free time
6:00	Practice IBNO
8:00	Evening Devotion
9:00	Game time
11:00	Retire to Rooms
12:00	Lights Out

Sunday

8:00	Wake up
9:00	Clean up Pack
9:30	Morning Devotion

Say: "Good friends can help us overcome the stress we experience in the form of peer pressure. When we surround ourselves with people who know what we believe in and can help us be faithful in our relationships with God, then we are more likely to take a stand when trouble comes."

10:00 Saying No

What Would You Say?

Distribute the Feeling the Pressure handouts (page 51). Using the handout, lead the "What Would You Say" activity on page 22. Once you've completed the activity, lead a discussion using the debriefing questions on the same page.

10:30 Break

Break/Snack Time

11:00 Bible Study

Integrity 101 Bible Study

Lead the discussion about integrity and boundaries using the activity and questions on pages 22–23. Say: "When we go outside the boundaries that God set for us, we are not fully loving God nor our neighbors. God set those boundaries for us so that we wouldn't harm others and so that we would love them. God doesn't just say, 'Don't do this' and 'Don't do that.' God wants us to take on Christ's character—to love God with our whole selves and to love our neighbors as much as we love ourselves. God also wants our actions to be expressions of that love—to be honest and to demonstrate integrity.

Distribute writing paper and pens. Have the youth write a letter to God expressing their thoughts about integrity and peer pressure. Encourage them to make this a conversation about what God is saying to them and what they might feel called to do about the pressures they face.

12:00 Closing

Conclude the retreat using the Christ candle or by using the worship plan on pages 63–64.

Closing

Conclude the retreat by standing together in a circle. Light a Christ candle and spend a few minutes talking with youth about what God may be calling them (and you) to do about the pressures they face. Say, "Ask yourselves: How will you go from this retreat and be a force for positive peer pressure at your school? How will you live a life of integrity?" After everyone has shared, begin the "The Challenge to Be Me" worship service on pages 63–64.

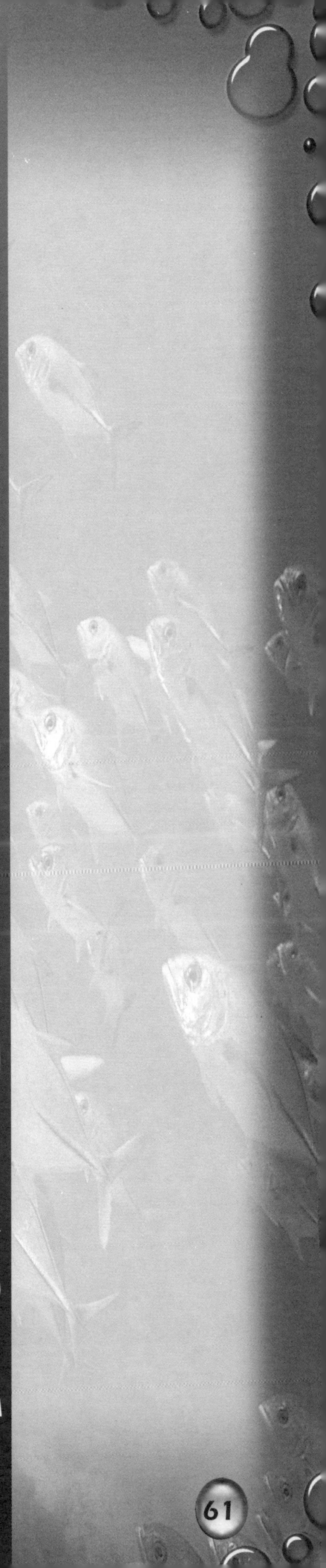

OUT AND ABOUT: Getting Out of Old Cliques

Topic: **Spending Time in Other People's Cliques**

Purpose: To help youth understand the dynamics of their youth group as well as the different interests of various cliques. By spending a day in new places and around different types of people, your youth will have a better understanding and, hopefully, appreciation for the differences.

Preparation

Take one day and visit as many different locations that are specific to as many different cliques as possible. Begin your day at a skating park, then attend an afternoon symphony, observe a debate if possible, then attend a sporting event. In the evening, consider stopping in a teen dance club before concluding the evening at an open-mic night at a bookstore. Remember to plan for meals between stops.

1. Decide on a date and time for your day of clique-hopping. Choose a day during which the most events are available. Saturday may be the best day for this event.
2. Decide which locations will get your group outside their particular boxes. If your group is made up of mostly jocks, spend the bulk of the day visiting non-sports related activities, but conclude the day with dinner and a sporting event. If you have mostly musicians, spend the day at a sporting event and top off the day by attending a symphony.
3. Organize a potential schedule of events, then check the schedule against actual activity times. Investigate admission fees and try to choose cost-free events. Keep the cost as low as possible.
4. Recruit some adult volunteers and drivers. Make sure they are covered under your church insurance policy.
5. Send home information fliers and permission forms at least two weeks in advance. Make sure that parents know what the day entails.

Out and About

1. Begin the day by saying: "Today, we are going to stretch our comfort zones and learn to appreciate a variety of interests. Our faith will grow

as we develop deeper friendships and learn why different people enjoy different activities. It's OK to be different! God made each of us unique and gave each of us various gifts and talents. Even if you are bored at some points today, try to experience the full range of interests and respect the fact that other people are having a good time. NO COMPLAINING!

"We are called to love our neighbors as ourselves, and that means sharing our lives together in Christ. Today is all about sharing our lives together! Let's go have some fun!"

2. Head out to your first destination!

3. Close the day by having dinner or coffee drinks at a local coffee-house. Use the following questions to motivate discussion:

   - How did it feel today to do something different—something you might have never tried?
   - What was your favorite activity?
   - How could more experiences like today's enrich our friendships and strengthen our youth group?
   - What happens when we set aside our images and really get to know one another—even those who seem very different than us?
   - How can you help your other friends look beyond your clique and care about "outsiders"?
   - What can we learn from today about the ways we respond to peer pressure?

   Close the discussion by saying: "We are all God's creation. We are all beautiful and loved completely by God. Because of that truth, we should love and respect one another as God's creations. Peer pressure can make us believe that we need to be like someone else or that we should do something we don't want to do. Jesus teaches that his love frees us from that mentality. We are free to live abundant lives in him—we don't have to give in to negative peer pressure. In fact, Christ calls us to stand tall in the crowd—to be in the world—but not of the world."

4. Conclude the evening by just hanging out and being together as a youth group.

Worship Service: The Challenge to Be Me

Scripture

"Love from the center of who you are; don't fake it. Run for dear life from evil; hold on for dear life to good. Be good friends who love deeply; practice playing second fiddle" (Romans 12:9-10, *Message).*

Opening Prayer

Say: "God, we welcome you to our lives. Our lives are different from when our parents were our ages. We are pressured to grow up fast and to deal with drugs, alcohol, and sex. We are growing and discovering who we are. We want to belong and be a part of the world, but we know that you call us to be in the world—not of the world. We want to grow in our Christian faith and to discover how to be faithful in the midst of the pressures of our lives. We recognize your love for us and the love of our families and church. We need your guidance and nurture to become all that you intend for us to be. Amen." Say something like: "Let us worship together, young and old, and discover the riches of God's love and plan for our lives."

Play worship music as youth enter the room.

Welcome Songs

- "God of Wonders" (*City on a Hill*)
- "Better Is One Day in Your Courts" (*Passion: Better Is One Day*)
- "Sanctuary" (found in most praise and worship songbooks)

Call to Worship

Leader: God is calling us to worship.
Youth: We are the people of God.
Leader: God is calling us to worship.
Youth: We are God's children.
Leader: God is calling us to be like Christ.
Youth: God knows our name and loves us as no other.

Sing a hymn of praise: "Amazing Grace" (or another familiar hymn).

Call to Confession

Say: "We are pushed on all sides to go with the flow. The world calls us to look a certain way, to be the first and best at everything, to assume that being humble means being weak. God calls us to live as Christ lived—to be last and use humility as a strength."

Prayer of Confession

Say: "God, we confess that we have been too easily swayed by negative peer pressure. We have not taken a stand often enough and not spoken out when you've nudged us. Forgive us for those times and help us depend on you as we overcome negative peer pressure and share your love with our friends. Amen."

Words of Assurance and Forgiveness

Leader: God calls us God's children. Abundant life is free in Christ Jesus.

Youth: We belong to God.

Leader: God has saved us from being bound to the world.

Youth: In Christ we are free indeed! Amen!

Time of Silent Confession

Play soft music and encourage youth to be silent. Say, "God wants to tell our hearts that we do, indeed, belong to the Heavenly Father. Invite those who may want to kneel to do so.

Proclaiming the Word

Prior to the worship service, invite several youth to share testimonies about ways God has been speaking to them about finding their worth and identity in God, or about their friendships, peer pressure, and sharing Christ's love.

Read aloud Luke 9:25. (Use *The Message* translation, if possible.) Call on the preenlisted youth to share their testimonies.

Response to the Word

Provide paper and pens.

Plan to play soft background music while youth write their conversations with God

Sing one of your group's favorite praise songs as a response to the shared testimonies.

As a response activity, hand out paper and pens. Ask youth to write IBNO at the top of their papers. Allow time for youth to list ways they will work to be in the world—but not of the world. Encourage them to have a conversation with God about how they are to live as Christians in this world. Instruct youth to fold their papers and place them on the altar as they feel led.

Holy Communion

You may choose to celebrate Holy Communion as a closing act of community and commitment. Celebrate this as your tradition requires, but allow the youth to serve one another. When everyone has been served, gather youth into a circle and lead them in a popcorn prayer. Sing "We Are the Body of Christ" or another favorite communion hymn or praise song.

Benediction with Blessing

Read aloud Romans 12:9-10 from the previous page.